SWINDLED NEVER AFTER

HOW WE SURVIVED
(AND YOU CAN SPOT)
A RELATIONSHIP SCAMMER

CECILIE FJELLHØY & PERNILLA SJÖHOLM

Podium

All rights reserved. No part of this publication may be reproduced, stored in a retrieval system, or transmitted in any form or by any means electronic, mechanical, photocopying, recording, or otherwise without prior written permission from Podium Publishing.

This is a work of fiction. Names, characters, places, and incidents are either products of the author's imagination or used fictitiously. Any resemblance to actual events, locales, or persons, living, dead, or undead, is entirely coincidental.

Copyright © 2025 by Cecilie Fjellhøy and Pernilla Sjöholm

Cover design by Faceout Studio

ISBN: 978-1-0394-8895-3

Published in 2025 by Podium Publishing
www.podiumentertainment.com

*To all victims hurting in shame and darkness:
you are seen, you are heard, and you matter.*

*To those fighting against fraud:
your efforts pave the way for change and offer us hope.*

Contents

Introduction	3

PART I THE SCAM

Chapter 1 What Victims Look Like	7
Chapter 2 Once Upon an App (How It All Began)	27
Chapter 3 Social Proof: Meet the Accomplices	44
Chapter 4 Emotional Grooming	62
Chapter 5 Plot Twist	88

PART II FIGHTING BACK

Chapter 6 Law Enforcement	121
Chapter 7 Financial Institutions	149
Chapter 8 The Media	172
Chapter 9 The World Is Changing (and So Are We)	189
Resources	214
Acknowledgments	217
About the Author	221

This book includes exact transcriptions of social media interactions, text messages, emails, and other online communication between the authors and various parties, which at times include typos, usage errors, and other mistakes.

SWINDLED
NEVER
AFTER

All fairy-tale friendships start somewhere, but our origin story was a real doozy. We met against the backdrop of a mutual nightmare, one you likely heard about and possibly watched from the comfort of your couch. *The Tinder Swindler*, Netflix's second most viewed documentary ever, tells the story of Simon Leviev (real name Shimon Hayut) defrauding us out of a collective $300,000 (and that's just a fraction of the over $10 million he's believed to have stolen from his victims from around the world). But the documentary didn't tell the whole story. In fact, it left out the best parts.

Here we reveal some of the shocking details and what-happened-next revelations viewers keep asking us about. But this book goes much deeper than us and our story—it exposes how and why the institutions we thought were there to protect us actually make it possible for fraudsters to continue getting away with their crimes. We interviewed experts from the psychology, law enforcement, and cybercrime sectors to help us unravel the complex layers of relationship fraud and concluded that society has been asking all the wrong questions.

When it comes to confidence fraud, we aren't good at pointing blame where it rightfully belongs. This reframe desperately matters because if society isn't examining the right problems, they'll continue to get the wrong solutions—or none at all—and there will continue to be victims of these crimes. Romance scams and other confidence schemes are among the world's fastest-growing frauds, causing $3.8 billion in losses globally in 2023, according to the Nasdaq 2024

Global Financial Crime Report*—and only a small percentage of these scams get reported. Based on the vitriol and judgment that came our way when we went public with our stories, we know why victims stay quiet. They're blamed, criticized, and persecuted for being complicit in their own con.

From "How could you fall for a scam?" to "Why didn't you catch him?" we have been asked all the wrong questions. But this is our chance to rewrite and reframe those questions to get to the real issues and provide solutions for societal change. We're about to flip everything you know about relationship fraud and the systems that fail fraud victims on its head and help you understand how these crimes *really* happen and how you can keep yourself and your loved ones safe.

Whether you simply saw the film and wondered *What happened next?*, are online dating and wanting to know what red flags to look out for (the key takeaways at the end of each chapter are for you!), are a victim of fraud—or suspect a loved one is—and are seeking to better understand what happened and how to heal (the Resources section in the back of the book provides support), or work in the law enforcement, banking, government, or big-tech sector and want to educate yourself and advocate for change within your organization when it comes to handling these kinds of situations, this book is for you.

No matter what brought you here, you will gain a new perspective from the inside on how fraud villains operate and what we as a society must do to stop them and provide support for victims.

---

* Nasdaq/Verafin, "2024 Global Financial Crime Report," accessed February 20, 2025, https://verafin.com/nasdaq-verafin-global-financial-crime-report/.

PART I
THE SCAM

How could you fall for a scam?
What makes a scam artist so believable?

CHAPTER 1

What Victims Look Like

~~What's wrong with you?~~
What's wrong with him?

Cecilie

The chaos in the room was familiar. A sense of anxiousness and anticipation. People sitting around, doing the same as me . . . waiting. Some staring into the air, moms calming their screaming children, a man wincing from a broken leg. Everyone hoping their name would be called next.

It was not my first time at Legevakten, the emergency hospital in Lillestrøm, my hometown outside Oslo, Norway. But this time I wasn't there for a physical illness or injury. My mom brought me there because she knew I was desperate. The kind of desperate that makes someone want to do something they can never, ever take back.

Just four months earlier, I seemingly had it all. By early 2018, I was finishing my master's degree in digital experience design, had just moved to London, and was working in a job that I loved, as a senior user experience (UX) designer. I was actively dating, mostly meeting men through dating apps, but I wasn't desperately looking for a romantic partner, and certainly not a sugar daddy; I was supporting myself just fine. I was happy and hopeful about my future. And then it all came crashing down. With a single swipe on someone's Tinder profile, and all the choices I made after, I managed to destroy my entire life. I had nine creditors relentlessly chasing me, showing no mercy, for the $250,000 in high-interest loan debt I had accumulated.

I was a victim of romance fraud.

How could this have happened to me? I seemed like such an unlikely victim. As a UX designer, I was trained to notice how people navigated websites and mobile apps; I was trained to observe people to uncover the truth of their behaviors. I worked in the tech world; I studied digital identity. I had even previously worked for a bank. I'd interviewed people in financial distress and knew the implications of maintaining good credit. I'd received awards for designing user technology that streamlined banking processes. Truly—how could I have fallen victim to financial fraud? If it could happen to me, I realized, it could happen to anyone.

I was raised in a country where I proudly believed I would get help when I needed it. I was naïve to the fact that the legal and public safety institutions that we think are there to protect us are nothing up against skilled manipulators and large corporations with deep pockets—especially when it comes to an emotional or financial crime rather than a physical crime. Instead, I was the one being blamed, questioned, suspected. *Can I bear this burden?* I thought. *Can my family bear it?* That was the part that hurt the most—the voicemail threat on my mother's home phone line from "Simon," the man who violated me, and the pain that my choices were causing those who loved me and whom I loved most.

It was May 2018. I was driving down the road in my hometown, alone with my thoughts for one of the first times since I'd realized I'd been defrauded. I thought about everything that was likely to pass. I couldn't bear having to tell the rest of my family what had happened, feeling their pain and sadness, telling friends and seeing their reactions, their disbelief and disappointment. *How could you do this, Cecilie?* The interviews with police and the distress of retelling everything that had happened to me. Facing society . . . people would see this as merely a situation of having been tricked by a boyfriend, rather than the serious crime that it was.

Looking at the list I had made of all the loans I had taken out made the situation I was in feel so real. These were huge sums of money. I needed a lawyer, but how could I afford one? The trouble I was in kept piling up. I would not be able to get the free legal help available in my country because the case was too intricate and involved several countries; most of the loans I had taken out were in Norway, but I lived and worked in the UK. The continued barrage of emails from creditors was enough to bury me. *This is going to be such an uphill battle*, I thought.

On top of all that, I was heartbroken. That's the piece people forget about. I was not given any time to mourn the loss of my relationship with a man—fake identity or not—whom I loved with all my heart, who turned around and showed me that he didn't give two shits about me. The man who held me in his arms, kissed me on the forehead, shared a bed with me, and planned a future with me . . . all of that was a lie. That is what makes me tear up, even today. It is still very painful to me that someone could be that evil . . . and that I ruined my own life for him. I had no time to process what had happened to me or to try to understand it or heal from it, because of all the practicalities that had to be dealt with. Outside of my family, all anyone wanted to discuss was the money. What about what I'd been through? Why weren't we discussing why I'd given him the money? How could this person manipulate and groom a person into ruining their own life? Hell, even I didn't understand how I could have done what I did at the time. *What a fool I have been*, I thought.

It was those thoughts I held in my head when driving down the road, alone at night. I felt like I was drowning; someone was dragging me to rock bottom. All of this, while my violator was still out there, living his life. It was dark and lightly raining. The streetlights were flickering. The headlights of a tractor-trailer coming toward me in the opposite lane were bright, enticing. *What if I turned the steering wheel?* I thought. *Wouldn't it be better to just end it here?*

Somehow, I pulled my focus back on the road and continue driving to my mom's house. She had never seen me so distraught. I told her about the thoughts I'd had in the car, and she immediately drove me to the emergency clinic. From there, I was referred to the acute psychiatric ward. Never, ever in my life had I thought I would end up in a mental institution. I felt so much shame; not only had I messed up my own life, but now my mom was having to take care of her thirty-year-old daughter.

I arrived at the psychiatric ward feeling like I could finally let go of the weight I was carrying. Once I got settled, I hugged my mother goodbye, tears pouring down my face. She held me tightly. "This is for your own good, Cecilie. You'll be safe now." After she left, I was given a sleeping aid and anxiety medication to calm down. Finally, I could sleep. I was so, so tired. Even before I realized I'd been defrauded, I hadn't been able to sleep because of constant communication from my fraudster. He had been calling day and night asking for more money, until I finally blocked him.

I was so grateful I had been able to keep my phone in the psychiatric ward because there was otherwise nothing to do; my phone was my lifeline to my mother and my friends and any sense of normalcy. At the same time, however, it was also dangerous to my mental health. I was receiving a constant deluge of emails from the banks, denying my requests for a grace period, demanding immediate payments. I would also get calls from *No Caller ID*, which I still don't answer to this day for fear that it's Simon calling from unknown numbers to threaten me some more. The police would also make calls this way, however, so I would miss their calls. As much as I needed to be at the facility, I worried that nothing was getting resolved during my stay. I was stuck in purgatory, unable to do anything to put my life back together.

But even greater than the financial scars he had left me with were the scars upon my mind and even my body. "We're going to need to take some blood samples," the nurse told me. Since I'd had a sexual relationship with Simon—someone whose every word to me had been a lie—there was no telling what type of disease I might have picked up from him. That was a horrible realization. *What has he done to my body?* I was so ashamed and embarrassed. I remember the anxiety I felt, waiting for the results of those tests to come back, and the relief I felt when I learned I was disease-free. Romance fraud is big business, yet what I don't hear the media, police, and society talking about is the fact that this type of fraud is so much more serious than just financial fraud. This isn't about a scammer calling us up and stealing our bank account information. Romance fraud violators (at least the in-person kind) sometimes invade our bodies . . . the most emotional and vulnerable aspects of ourselves. By not talking about this part, we're ignoring why this type of fraud hurts even more. We had a physical, intimate connection with our violators, who were so skilled at their crime that we felt they were not our violator but our protector. Talk about messing with your mind.

I ended up staying in acute care for five days. The care I received was exactly what I needed to start regaining some strength to take on the necessary next steps. I had been beaten down so much, I needed a proper breather.

Looking back on that time now, I feel so sad for myself. I shouldn't have gotten to the point where I had to check myself into a psych ward. If I had been properly supported by the police as a victim, if the banks had agreed to give me a grace period of even a month so I could gather my thoughts, that would have made all the difference. I wouldn't have felt such pressure . . . the feeling that I was going to lose everything now if I didn't take action immediately. I wouldn't have been driven to consider taking my own life.

I went to therapy long after that crisis episode because the risk is always still there. I'm still on antidepressants. But now I get sadder over others who were victims of crimes and felt like they had no way out but to take their own life than I do for myself. If I had not had the support of my family and friends, and Norway's and the UK's mental healthcare systems, I could have been one of them. I cry over what I went through, too, but I'm happy that I am still here.

What I can't get my head around is that, to this day, the man who violated me is still out there, scamming more victims. I knew, even back when I was in acute care, that he had other victims lined up after me. My bank statements had shown the names of women whose flights he'd purchased, who were being groomed to be defrauded. I'd asked the bank representative if I could contact the women, but they insisted they were working on a big case and that contacting them would interfere with their investigations.

"But you will contact them, right?" I asked.

"Yes, we will contact them." I was satisfied with that answer. I trusted that the banks and law enforcement were taking responsibility for protecting the other victims-to-be. That was foolish of me, considering how unprotected I had been. Cecilie of today would have ignored their advice and contacted the other women, hopefully before they were defrauded. But at the time, I had nine creditors to deal with, police who (spoiler alert) started investigating me as a suspect in my own crime, a lawyer to find who would be willing to take on my case, and court trials on the horizon.

Eight months later, over in Sweden, Pernilla Sjöholm—one of the names that was on my bank statements—would struggle with the realization that her new friend Simon wasn't who she thought he was . . . and her life would never be the same.

Pernilla

Before I met Simon in March 2018, I believed myself able to sense an untrustworthy person; it was my special talent, I said, to spot a liar. On the rare occasions when I bumped into people with sociopathic or narcissistic traits, I kept my distance. I'd never been put to the test quite like this, though.

Until then, my life had been pretty idyllic. I was born in Stockholm, Sweden; I grew up in a house by a lake and spent my summers swimming and horseback riding. My family is very tight; my cousins are almost like my siblings. We're very loving, caring, and trusting people. My parents modeled a healthy, loving relationship as well as the importance of hard work. My dad is a police officer who had previously worked for Europol—the European Union's (EU's) law enforcement agency for combating international crime, terrorism, and cybercrime. My mom is an entrepreneur who owned her own restaurant chain as well as an ambulance company, through which she educated emergency staff.

I am a very down-to-earth, hardworking, and social person; my romantic relationships have been mostly long-term, healthy, and stable, and my friendships close. I started managing restaurants in my early twenties, followed by working in company sales. Early on, I began investing in the stock market and real estate and am financially savvy. Fiercely independent, I worked hard to save up enough money to buy my own flat at age twenty-three. Since I worked in fields where I was surrounded by men who were older than me, I became comfortable asserting myself, ready to take on being challenged. Which is why I'm shocked that I didn't see Simon coming.

In January 2019, I was at a vendor fair for my sales job when I received a message from a newspaper journalist in Norway, confirming that Simon was a scammer, something I had been just starting to realize, and I was likely a victim. My worst fears came to life. The wire transfer Simon had sent to pay back a "loan" I had given him—that I was waiting to be accepted by my bank—was never going to go through. My head was spinning. I felt a fever come over me and almost passed out. Until then, I had a good life . . . a great life. On a whim, I could fly internationally to meet a friend. I happily treated my friends and family to nice dinners and holidays. I was so proud to be independent. Now I'd lost all my savings, including the money I had made on the recent sale of my flat that I was going to use to buy a new apartment. *My entire life is ruined*, I thought.

I went to the police station the next day. I was so angry, especially when I'd been told that this had happened to someone else—that a victim in Norway had my name and knew I was going to be the next target. The police and the banks also had my name and knew I was going to be the next victim. Even the reporters from this magazine had known about me for months. And no one bothered to give me a five-second fucking phone call to warn me! I thought. That was the hardest hit for me—more than being defrauded. I felt like my life was worth nothing; no one cared about what was going to happen to me. I felt abused—mentally, spiritually, and even physically, down to my bones.

Money is an important aspect of fraud, but not the most important. Although we'd met on Tinder, Simon and I did not have a romantic relationship. However, I was a victim of relationship fraud. He'd built a friendship with me, with the intention of defrauding me of huge sums of money. He and his fraud partners left me feeling worthless, shattered. My entire body hurt; my heart hurt. I got rashes all over my body. I was in shock.

I had so many regrets. How could I let this happen? How could I have been so used? I was also thinking, *What have I done to deserve this in life?* I started doubting what I loved about myself—that I am a caring person who always puts others before me. My dad always said to me, "Pernilla, you are very intelligent, but you listen too much with your heart instead of your brain." When I love and trust someone, I want to help them. But my dad now seemed right. My caring comes at a cost.

I'd been taught the difference between right and wrong, and that we should always help people when we can. I don't like seeing people sad or struggling. Although I loved Disney movies, I wasn't the kid who dressed up as a princess. I dressed up as Batman, ready to save the world. I fell victim to my own sense of decency. My goodness was taken advantage of. I lost my savings to a man who had become one of my best friends over the course of nine months. Only, he didn't really exist. None of his friends, whom I'd hung out with as well, were real either. I found myself wondering, who were they all, really? And what were they capable of?

I had no idea what to do; I felt so worthless, I became suicidal. Not only did I not know what I would do to myself, I didn't know what Simon might try to do to me. The death threats I received after I confronted him were not cryptic; they were spoken as if they were a done deal: "I've paid a price for your head. It wasn't even that expensive—it only cost a thousand euros because you aren't worth anymore."

I was scared to go out. I was looking over my shoulder, looking under my car to see if there could be a bomb under it. I feared for not only my life but those of the people I loved. I didn't want to meet with friends; I didn't dare visit my grandma and grandpa's house, because I was so scared that something would happen to them. I never felt so bad my entire life. I didn't go through with the idea of killing myself, but the only version of myself that I'd ever known—that of a trusting, caring, fun-loving individual? That Pernilla died.

THE RISE OF RELATIONSHIP FRAUD

What is relationship fraud, anyway? Relationship fraud, also known as confidence fraud, dating or romance fraud, or "sweetheart swindles," refers to situations where a person is defrauded by an offender through what the victim perceives to be a genuine relationship. Offenders use the façade of an (often romantic) relationship to cultivate trust and rapport with victims, for the sole purpose of deceiving and manipulating their targets into sending money.

Fraudsters could be individuals acting alone or as part of an organized crime group, operating domestically or internationally. The fraudsters often hide behind fake documents and use their victims' money across complex networks. Just like we have the education, training, and personality traits to be very good at our jobs, so too do fraudsters have the unique skills and characteristics to be very good at what they do. They are professional criminals; it is their full-time job to scam us. They create fake profiles (sometimes with stolen images, and more recently with AI-generated images) and search dating sites, apps, and social media platforms for victims, then maintain long-term relationships (often, several at once) based on lies that are specific to each individual victim. They work to quickly build trusting relationships that could be familial, friendly, or romantic, while seeming genuine, caring, and believable. All the while they are skillfully using language to manipulate, persuade, and exploit their victims.

We interviewed Dr. Elisabeth Carter, a UK criminologist and forensic linguist, for further insight into the psychology behind scams.

FROM A CRIMINOLOGIST'S PERSPECTIVE: DR. ELISABETH CARTER

Romance fraudsters use a variety of different techniques—some of which are simple, and some of which are not—that are designed to get their victims to do things without realizing what they're doing. The victim becomes so ingrained in this non-reality that they don't see the cage they are inside; even in hindsight, it can look like a cage of their own making. The whole scam is designed to make the victim feel responsible, when they're not. In a way, it's a perfect crime.

How fraudsters distort their victims' perception of reality is aligned with grooming tactics used in cases of domestic abuse and coercive control, such as gaslighting and "creeping normality." These two forms of manipulation both involve the perpetrator using visceral responses that are designed to make the victim feel responsible for their psychological or physical distress and draw a protective response toward the fraudster, which will then be used to extort money from the victim.

Creeping normality is a term used in romance-based communications for the slow progression of deception that eventually leads the victim to send money to the perpetrator. One of the big misunderstandings about romance fraud is the perception that criminals demand money out of the blue; what in fact happens is the perpetrator will groom the victim into believing the relationship is real and leave no red flags signaling that the relationship is anything other than real. They use the context of the relationship to enact tactics of manipulation, such as framing requests for secrecy as romantic—"just us against the world"—and that sharing information with others about the relationship is being untrustworthy and inappropriate. Requests for money often appear as the perpetrator showing that they are struggling, and that financial help would ease their struggle, leading victims to offer assistance.

Onlookers at this stage may find it unbelievable what the victim is willing to believe; however, by the time the victim gives money to the perpetrator, they have been groomed into thinking they are making good, reasonable, and rational decisions but are in fact operating in an alternate reality that has been created by the perpetrator and is impossible for the victim to distinguish from reality or believe it is not real.

The priming of victims to give money to the perpetrator is done by framing money as something other than money: as a gift, as something to assist the relationship, as a joint enterprise, as a small additional amount of money to add to the money the victim has already paid, or as something that will stop some psychological or physical harm to the perpetrator. The victim is made to feel in control, and feels as though they want to support, help, and protect the perpetrator.

***

Together, these tactics can lead victims to financial and emotional ruin. The fraudster's lies can cause severe anxiety. In our case, Simon's demands were shrouded in a safety narrative. He fabricated a perceived threat to his life that validated his urgency for secrecy. This isolated his victims from their family and friends and made them reliant on him for human connection—the only one who "understands." The fraudster must strike a balance between the relational and financial aspects of their communication for their criminal intent to remain hidden, being careful not to set off alarm bells when asking for money by maintaining stories and dropping pieces of information over months or even years (the long game is where the big bucks are). The victim is likely to experience a decline in decision-making capabilities simply because of their extended exposure to the fraudster and their stories.

Relationship fraud is big business (cybercrime as a whole is the world's third largest economy).* Our perpetrator alone has been reported to have swindled women (and men) out of several million

---

* Cybernews, "Cybercrime Is World's Third-Largest Economy Thanks to Booming Black Market," February 3, 2023, https://cybernews.com/editorial/cybercrime-world-third-economy/.

dollars between 2017 and 2019 alone. That is just one man. Romance fraud has a devastating impact on thousands of people globally each year. Consider these stats for scope:

- Between January 2020 and December 2024, UK residents reported nearly 40,000 cases of romance fraud, resulting in financial losses exceeding £400 million, with Londoners being the most affected group, accounting for over 5,000 reports.*
- In 2024, nearly 59,000 Americans reported losing a total of $697.3 million to romance scams, with a median loss of approximately $2,000 per victim.**
- Canadians reported losing over $58.4 million to romance fraud and $310 million to investment fraud in 2024, with some romance scams linked to cryptocurrency schemes that further amplify victims' financial losses.***
- In 2024 an estimated US$1.03 trillion has been lost to scams worldwide.****

---

* *London Daily News*. "Londoners Hit Hardest by Dating Scams as Estimated Cost of Romance Fraud Tops £400 Million." Written by *London Daily News* Staff. Published March 30, 2025. www.londondaily.news/londoners-hit-hardest-by-dating-scams-as-estimated-cost-of-romance-fraud-tops-400-million/ (accessed April 3, 2025).
** Comparitech. "Romance Scams: How to Spot Them and Protect Yourself." Written by Comparitech Staff. Published March 25, 2025. www.comparitech.com/blog/vpn-privacy/romance-scams/ (accessed April 3, 2025).
*** *Canadian Fraud News*. "Think You Can Spot a Romance Scam? Canadians Lost More Than $58 Million Last Year After Being Led Into Web of Lies." Written by *Canadian Fraud News* Staff. Published March 28, 2025. www.canadianfraudnews.com/think-you-can-spot-a-romance-scam-canadians-lost-more-than-58-million-last-year-after-being-led-into-web-of-lies/ (accessed April 3, 2025).
**** GASA and Feedzai. "The Global State of Scams Report 2024." Written by Feedzai Staff. Published 2024. www.feedzai.com/resource/global-state-of-scams-report-2024/ (accessed April 3, 2025).

But those are just soulless numbers. In cases of relationship fraud, we rarely see beyond the numbers or dollar signs and examine the psychological harm. There's no way to quantify the emotional damage that relationship fraud does to its victims—which also leads to this type of crime being grossly underreported. The Federal Bureau of Investigation (FBI) estimates that as few as 15 percent of these crimes are reported, while the CAFC estimates their figure to be less than 10 percent of the crimes that actually occur. Similar to victims of sexual abuse, most victims are too embarrassed, too distraught, too scared, too *something* to come forward. Their perpetrator may have threatened them; they may have heard stories of how other victims were treated like criminals by the institutions we thought were put in place to protect us, or they might see on social media how other victims have been blamed and shamed for their actions—or inactions—and decided *Nope, not going through that*.

The psychological impact was going on long before the money was lost, and it continues long after.

THE EMOTIONAL IMPACT OF FRAUD

Fraud victims are a unique lot. Stacey Wood, a psychologist at Scripps College and co-editor of the book *A Fresh Look at Fraud*, published in 2022, told NBC News* that they are more likely to blame themselves (and be blamed by others) than victims of other crimes. Robbery victims, for example, don't tend to question their own intelligence, decision-making, or self-worth. They are also more likely to get sympathy and support from others. Fraud victims are much more likely to feel embarrassed and ashamed and uncomfortable talking about their experience. These emotions can lead to depression, panic attacks, trouble sleeping, inability to concentrate, post-traumatic stress disorder (PTSD), and even suicide.

---

* Herb Weisbaum, "Not Just a Financial Toll: Some Victims of Identity Theft Consider Suicide," NBC News, November 6, 2017, https://www.nbcnews.com/news/amp/ncna817966.

The AARP Fraud Watch Network's director of victim support, Amy Nofziger, who oversees the toll-free helpline (877-908-3360), says that callers frequently tell their trained volunteers, "I don't know what else to do. I might as well just kill myself." There are no statistics on the number of people who have died by suicide after a scam, but we have plenty of anecdotal evidence. We receive frequent messages from victims or family members of victims who have attended our talks or seen the documentary *The Tinder Swindler* and reached out to tell us they have thought about suicide themselves or lost a loved one to suicide. These messages break our hearts.

> Now I've lost $120k, and I don't know what to do. It was my life savings, I spent 4.5 years saving it all. I feel like my life is over.

> I am so stupid. I am so ashamed, embarrassed, hurt, and angry. But mostly stupid. I have thought that I have no business being allowed to live.

> They scammed me with $70K, I have a daughter, the bank in a few months will take my house and my car for not being able to pay the debts. I need advice from you, my soul is shattered.

In addition to the amount of money lost in relation to a victim's overall budget or financial situation, a factor that can affect the extent of a victim's trauma is if another person, such as a spouse or other family member, is financially or emotionally impacted by the victim having been scammed. The victim's sense of responsibility is therefore compounded, which is something we experienced ourselves. We felt worse about how our choices impacted our parents and grandparents' health and safety than how they impacted us.

Christine Kieffer, senior director at the FINRA Investor Education Foundation, emphasized that grief can be deepest for victims of romance scams. "We all know that when you break up with somebody, even when on good terms, there's a sense of loss. So, imagine what you'd feel like if it was all built on lies," she said.* She added that scam victims are often more isolated after the crime; some victims lose friendships because they have dedicated so much time to building a relationship with their scammer, or from having cut friends out of their lives who challenged the new relationship. Suddenly, at the moment when victims need emotional support most, their friends are no longer there. Support is critical for healing to begin, yet many scam victims keep silent about their experience for years, allowing the trauma to fester.

Of course, our emotional health affects our physical health as well. Scam victims have reported losing weight, escalating drinking or smoking habits, developing high blood pressure . . . and then, for those who had a sexual relationship with their perpetrator, victims are at risk of contracting sexually transmitted diseases (STDs). The list of impacts is seemingly never-ending. Our very lives are threatened, our futures at stake.

Over time, we may start to recover our emotional or physical health, but reminders of what happened to us are always lurking, in the background or foreground. Our lifestyles are likely to have been significantly impacted as a result of devastating financial losses; we may have trouble getting credit cards or loans, and therefore trouble buying a home or even renting.

These moments are hard. But we are not alone. Support is out there. And remember: if you've been a victim of a scam, *it's not your fault*.

YES, THIS COULD HAPPEN TO YOU

Sadly, a common reaction to relationship fraud cases is to focus on the perceived naïveté, foolishness, and culpability of the victim. Believe us, we've heard it all.

---

* Christina Ianzito, "Many Victims Struggle with Mental Health in Scams' Aftermath," AARP, December 15, 2022, https://www.aarp.org/money/scams-fraud/info-2022/mental-health-impact.html.

> I loved watching you cry on national television for being a gold digger so much. You are a prime example why dating is the way it is.

> Sorry but you're such a naive person. It's not Simon's fault what's happened - it's yours for being a naive person.

> Over 1000 matches on Tinder ,Over 7 years Single, And she wanna tell us she's no GOLD DIGGER but it was true love

> Women can be damn stupid sometimes. A fool and her money...

> Poor gold digger - be happy its not punishable to be stupid, you would be put in jail for LIFE!

But what many people don't see, or understand, is that a skilled con artist can lead anyone to become a victim, given the "right" cues. If you haven't been exposed to grooming processes before, it can be hard to believe that it could happen to you. *But relationship fraud can happen to anybody*—people of all genders, ages, sexual orientations, and cultural backgrounds. Interestingly, men and women are almost equally targeted by relationship fraudsters, despite misconceptions that there are more female victims than male.

Research psychologists Daniel Simons and Christopher Chabris, authors of *Nobody's Fool: Why We Get Taken In and What We Can Do about It*,* told us how, with the rise of true crime stories in the media, the public thinks they could spot red flags in their own life, because those warnings seemed so easily identifiable in the story they heard. But this is because they already knew what they were watching or reading about was a scam. "It's like trying to solve a mystery when you already know who committed the crime," Chabris explained. "It is much easier

---

* Daniel Simons and Christopher Chabris, interview with authors, July 29, 2024.

after the fact to identify red flags and look for the hints and suggestions that could have tripped somebody up. Therefore, the media reinforces the idea that we are too smart to be scammed ourselves."

Research psychologist Maria Konnikova, author of *The Confidence Game*, echoes Simons and Chabris. As she told *Business Insider*,* "Sometimes people who are more intelligent actually make even better victims than people who aren't quite as sophisticated or as educated." If you think you're immune, that you're too clever to fall for a scam, then you're actually the perfect mark—you're *over*confident.

As much as we may not like to admit it or can't yet see it, Chabris states, "Every single person has already been conned or scammed or misinformed or deceived in some way. There's a lot of political misinformation going around, for example. Maybe we haven't given away our life savings with a Ponzi scheme or wired all our money to a romance fraudster, but I think we've all been involved in the same process in some way."

Still think this couldn't happen to you? We get it. Before we got scammed, we thought we were too intelligent, too worldly, too savvy to be conned. Financial scams only happened to older, wealthy people with declining cognitive abilities, right?

When we met Simon, we were well-traveled women with big careers. Smart, confident, high-performing people. We weren't hopelessly lonely, or desperate, or willing to do anything to keep a man interested or a friendship intact. We were quite normal women with normal dating histories. We were also financially independent; we had purchased our own homes and didn't come from trust fund families. Everything we had, we'd built ourselves. We also had pretty high standards for relationships because we'd already seen a thing or two. Simon didn't provide anything special per se other than the right words at the right time, amplified by a complex network and skilled manipulation.

---

* Richard Feloni, "Psychologist: Being Smart Could Make You More Prone to Fall for a Con Artist's Lies," *Business Insider*, March 24, 2016, https://www.businessinsider.com/why-you-cant-be-too-smart-for-a-con-artist-2016-3.

If you have only one takeaway from this chapter, let it be this: *There's no such thing as being too intelligent to be conned.* Now, it's true: if you're feeling isolated or lonely, or going through a job loss, divorce, serious injury, or a downturn in finances, you're likely to be more vulnerable to becoming a victim of fraud. In other words, it's not who you are but where you happen to be at the particular moment in your life when a confidence artist approaches that can make you particularly vulnerable. Interestingly, the simple act of "looking for love" makes a person more vulnerable, since we have to be open and trusting to fall in love. Even so, an overarching victim profile does not exist. Even looking for traits that make someone "susceptible" to fraud dances a fine line of blaming the victim instead of acknowledging what makes the con artist so successful.

So, what do victims look like? Like us, but also like you. Often, victims are the most empathetic, kind, patient, respectful, trusting, and generous people. The kinds of people we want in our lives as friends and partners . . . someone who cares and will help us out when we most need them. These aren't people we should be attacking; these are the kinds of people we need more of in this world. We hope that by sharing our stories, we are not only helping others avoid victimization but helping to put an end to victim shaming and blaming. We are victims of not just fraud but abuse.

We are not here to scare you. We know that being online today, especially while searching for a partner, can be intimidating. Fraud is now one of the most common crimes in the world—not exactly a confidence-boosting fact. We are often asked, "Did you stop using dating apps after your experience?" No! We didn't stop believing in love, either. How tragic it would be if we were to give Simon the power to take *that* away from us, too. Instead, we've used our experiences, and everything we've learned about fraud thereafter, to arm ourselves to become experts in our own right on what to look out for, so we—and you—know how to spot a relationship scammer and can simply enjoy falling in love.

HOT TIPS

- If you think you're too clever to fall for a scam, then you're actually the perfect mark.

- Check for fake passports, documents, and online profiles (double, even triple, verify!).

- Don't wait too long to ask questions; once you've been pulled in, it's much harder to take a step back and notice the questions you should have asked.

- Beware of someone who demands secrecy about their situation or who isolates you from family and friends. They may use phrases such as "you are the only one who understands" in order to isolate and manipulate you.

- If somebody asks for money, no matter at what stage in a relationship (especially if they're asking for more and more), that's a red flag.

- Asking somebody neutral for their viewpoint is often one of the best ways to avoid being scammed.

CHAPTER 2

Once Upon an App (How It All Began)

~~Weren't you just attracted to Simon's wealth?~~
How did Simon make himself attractive to you?

Say we set you up on two dates with two different people, one of whom is a con artist. We give you the full name of both your dates, so you can Google your little heart out before you go. On a scale of 1 to 10, how confident are you that you could correctly identify the con artist once you've done this and then gone on the dates?

If we'd been asked this a few years ago, our numbers would have been high. Super high. If we had both verified every detail that we knew about Simon from Tinder before we went out with him, it would have checked out. His name was Simon Leviev (Instagram, check!). He worked for LLD Diamonds (LinkedIn, check!). His business was legit (articles online about the company and the Leviev family, check!). His basic details were all easily verifiable . . . which is why we never would have considered that a skilled con artist was on the other side of our Tinder app.

Meeting him in person—and then meeting his friends, family (his daughter), and business associates—added to our confidence. Getting defrauded by Simon Leviev started with *believing* him. Whether someone is swindling you out of money over the internet, in an investment scheme, or through your relationship with them, they're taking important steps that engender trust and play on your human desire to believe that they are who they say they are.

There are a few strategies these individuals use to find their targets and make themselves seem believable in the beginning: They use social media to find their targets. They know their targets. They know how to appeal to their targets.

The result: a skillfully laid trap.

Cecilie

"Congratulations! You have a new match." It was January 13, 2018, and the countdown to my thirtieth birthday (less than four weeks away!) had started. It was a time of relative transition. I had just moved to London, which was far different from my hometown outside Oslo, Norway, in population, culture, and lifestyle. There was only one main road in the town where I grew up. It was a safe community of outdoor enthusiasts; as a child, I loved to go cross-country skiing. I thought that having a cinema made my town of twenty thousand a real metropolis; now in London, I was in a city of ten million, where it rarely snowed.

I was ready for my new life! I'd started a new job and enthusiastically begun matching with men on Tinder. My profile depicted a confident, intelligent, fun-loving, caring (and carefree), successful woman (or at least I hoped so). There were images of me jumping in front of a mountain in Zermatt, Switzerland; participating in Oslo's "bratteste" uphill running race; lying on a beach in West Palm Beach, Florida. Plus, some selfies. I love a good selfie; I was once dubbed "Selfilie" by my work colleagues (not that that is something to brag about!).

Swiping on dating apps can feel like a necessity for finding a date in the modern era, whether looking for casual fun or someone to settle down with. Or it can be pure entertainment. That particular Saturday night, I was swiping out of boredom, plain and simple. I'd been at home, diligently working on my master's thesis that I'd been procrastinating on forever. *I deserve a break*, I told myself. Lying on the sofa, I picked up my phone and opened Tinder. There were so many men in London! I saw dating apps as opportunities to meet people I normally wouldn't cross paths with.

It wasn't long before I landed on "Simon, 32." His profile, like mine, was very telling through photos. *Now, this guy looks interesting*, I thought. There were photos of him sitting in the back of a fancy car, lounging in a private jet, dining out while dressed in designer clothes. He was a businessman; I could tell that he worked in the diamond industry (Leviev is quite a famous name, if you Google it). *This would be a fun guy to go on a date with*, I thought. *He will have some stories to tell.*

I knew nothing about his world or this lifestyle. I hadn't ever been on a date with a finance guy. Simon clearly preferred urban life, going out to clubs, and eating at expensive restaurants. He was my type, physically: dark hair (Norwegians are always blond!), dark skin, facial hair, brown eyes. *I wonder what he's like behind the pictures*, I thought.

Swipe right. It was a quick decision.

It wasn't long before I received notice that we were a match. What Simon probably saw in me was a good target for his scam: someone who was not financially needy, didn't have an established local network of friends or family, enjoyed traveling and going out and having a good time. He may have also picked up on my impulsiveness and sense of adventure. He had a type, I would learn. He liked blondes and Scandinavian women (read: women from more trusting countries).

Still, it was me who made the first move after we'd been matched. "Something tells me you're not going to be in London for long ;)" I wrote, based on how much I saw that he traveled.

> Cecilie: Something tells me you're not going to be in London for long ;)

> Simon: I'm here every day I'm leaving tomorrow

> Cecilie: Too bad. You're coming back?

> Simon: Yes, maybe we can meet tomorrow for a coffee

> Cecilie: Yeah, I'm writing on my master thesis, delivering it on Wednesday, so I'm a bit stressed. So if you can handle that then it would be nice with a break

> Simon: Yes we can do it, tomorrow at 11

> Cecilie: I'm in! Where?

> Simon: In 4 Season Hotel Park Lane at the lobby. Text me on WhatsApp.

"I'm here every day, but I'm leaving tomorrow. Maybe we can meet tomorrow for a coffee?" Very quickly, he suggested moving the conversation off Tinder and over to WhatsApp. Despite it being crunch time for finishing my master's thesis, I again resolved that I deserved a short break from all the pressure. We made plans for coffee at ten thirty a.m. at the Four Seasons hotel, where he said he was staying.

My excitement made the tube ride the next morning feel like it lasted forever. Finally, I arrived. I entered the hotel lobby and looked around. It was posh, with dark red décor and tall glass windows. I always feel like I don't belong in these settings, especially since I had no intention of staying overnight at the hotel. *I almost feel like a fraud*, I thought. I took a seat on one of the red sofa chairs in the lobby and snapped a selfie.

I texted Simon the photo. "I'm here!" Shortly after, the hotel elevator dinged, and he came walking out. He radiated confidence, which I found very attractive. I walked toward him and saw that he wasn't very tall, but I've always said I can take the short kings.

We gave each other a quick hug. I noticed the Jewish kippah on his head; he stood out from other men in the religious sense, too, which further intrigued me and contributed to my level of trust in him. *He must have a very strong faith*, I thought.

He led me into the café and pulled out a chair for me to sit down. I had been nervous, but he had a calming energy about him that relaxed me. We ordered coffee and went through a series of standard questions. He was a proper gentleman; he listened more than he talked. I told him I was from Norway and a UX designer, about to finish my master's degree. "What kind of work do you do?" I asked.

"I'm in the diamond business. It's my father's company that I'm heading up," he said. "My dad's nickname is 'the king of diamonds,' so that makes me the prince," he said flirtatiously. "I'm trying to make him proud," he added. He was traveling around, wining and dining and courting clients, and signing deals. For someone like me from small-town Norway, it seemed like a stressful life, but of course exciting. "I'm growing tired of all of it, though," he added. "I want to settle down." I nodded and agreed I wanted to settle down, too. I was curious, however, about why he would portray the club and luxury lifestyle on his social media sites if he was looking for true love.

"Why are you so flashy about your wealth in all your photos online?

"It's my life, why should I hide it?" he answered.

"But aren't you scared of attracting the wrong type of people?" I countered.

"I am good at reading people," he said with a wink. He then revealed that he had a two-year-old daughter whom he totally adored and who was in London with her mother that weekend. "I'm really excited because I don't get to see my daughter that often," he said. I'd dated a guy with a child once before and was nervous about doing so again, but the way that Simon was gushing about his daughter allowed me to see the family side of him. *He's sweet*, I thought. *He really loves his daughter.* I didn't feel threatened by this other woman, because he explained they'd only had a "one-night stand in Bangkok."

He had made a mistake but was doing the responsible thing and caring for his child.

Just as I had suspected, we had tons to talk about. Before long, he looked at me with the biggest smile and said, "I would love to spend more time with you. This has been too short."

"I feel the same. When will you be back?"

"I'm not sure, but we are flying to Bulgaria today on business. Would you like to come along?"

I laughed. "What? No, I can't." I pointed to my laptop bag. "I have my thesis I need to write today." I had planned to go straight to a café to work after our date.

"You can write on the plane," Simon retorted. "Please? It would be wonderful to have more time together, and I don't know exactly when I'll be back."

I looked at my laptop bag again, and back at Simon. I've always been the type of person who would rather regret something I did than something I didn't do, and I think Simon picked up on that. So, what's an adventurous girl to do?

"Okay. I'll join." I smiled.

He found me at the exact right time. I was entering a new phase of my life and was maybe a bit lonely. I wanted someone to experience life with who was sweet and fun and caring. I was in a big city in a new country, equal parts open to this new and exciting world and naïve to it. The stars were aligning, so to speak, but it turns out more in his favor than in mine.

Pernilla

When I met Simon in March 2018, I was thirty-one years old and coming off a seven-year relationship. Even though I was newly single, I didn't feel vulnerable. I wasn't lonely or sad or desperate for anything. I was happy, but I did want to meet someone with whom I could live everyday life, someone who was ambitious and spontaneous. Someone smart and inspiring, who could help me become a better version of myself. When I found that person, I wanted to get married and build a family. I had always been in long, committed relationships and was new to dating apps; they hadn't really existed or been popular at other times in my life when I was single (gosh, it sounds like I was born in the 1800s!).

"It's hard to meet people these days. You should try using Tinder," a friend suggested. I felt a bit skeptical at first, but decided, why not? Several of my friends had met their partners through dating apps. Maybe I could, too.

I love seeing the world and meeting people from other countries and was looking for someone who would share my sense of adventure. My online profiles featured photos of me traveling around Europe, wearing smart work clothes, enjoying nice meals out, and socializing with friends, mixed with a spice of nature.

Simon Leviev was one of the men I matched with during my first month on the app. His Tinder profile showed a similar lifestyle to mine. There were world-class hotels, rooftop parties, and extravagant meals. He clearly traveled a lot. He was a career man; he wore smart workwear and posted videos of professional business meetings. There was something aspirational and intriguing about him; he seemed to work hard but also enjoy life. His photos showed him surrounded by friends, which made him feel more real and likeable.

So when we matched on Tinder and he reached out to meet in person, I thought, *Sure, what is the worst that could happen?* I wasn't overly eager, however. He quickly suggested we move our conversations off Tinder and onto WhatsApp and invited me to join him for coffee, but I had work meetings that day and wasn't willing to move or miss them. Then he tried to get me to fly to Barcelona that evening on his private jet. Being invited to fly on a private jet was the perfect setup in hindsight, congruent to the fairy-tale stories we hear all the time, right? But it didn't impress me much, to be honest. Besides, I already had plans that night to meet up with friends, and I didn't want to cancel them to go off with a guy I'd never met.

We chatted and talked on the phone for another three weeks before he asked me to go see him in Amsterdam, where he said he was living at the time. "Since you're making the effort to meet me there, I will pay for your flight," he generously offered. I had friends in Amsterdam, so I figured that if we didn't hit it off, I could at least visit my friends. He asked for my passport details so he could book a flight for me from Stockholm to Amsterdam, where I'd spend two nights.

We made plans to meet at a trendy café in Amsterdam, which turned out to be in the same building as his multistory apartment. I took a taxi from the airport to the café. My first reaction as I watched Simon approach the car to pay the driver was that he seemed nervous or stressed; he was fumbling with his phone and credit card. But then he greeted me warmly and, after lunch and a glass of wine, I felt like we'd known each other for years.

During the meal, he asked a lot of questions and really listened to my answers. It felt rare to have a man listen; it's sad to say, in retrospect, that this could be a warning sign—a man asking too many questions! In the moment, however, it just felt like he cared. He knew I loved to travel, so he asked where I normally visited, what type of cuisine I liked, what I did for a living, what my family was like, what my goals in life were. To me, it felt like a nice, normal, getting-to-know-you conversation.

I asked questions about his life, too. He told me about how his family had cut off contact with him for a while because he had been reckless when young, and for not being such an orthodox Jew. He'd left Israel, moved to London, and met someone who got him a job in arms dealing. He became a successful businessman, which made his dad proud and healed their relationship to some extent, at which point his father invited him to join LLD Diamonds, the family business. He still wasn't that close to his family, he said. He told me that his parents were in Israel and his siblings in New York.

He also said that he had spent time in jail abroad for a business deal gone bad, after being set up by his business partners.

"What happened to your business partners?" I asked.

"I don't know, no one's seen them since," he said. I kind of laughed it off; his story seemed melodramatic.

"Do you want to come up and see my apartment?" he asked after lunch. "You can stay in one of the guest rooms, or I can check you into a hotel if you're more comfortable with that."

I agreed to see his apartment. When I entered, something didn't seem right; it was as if he weren't really living there. It seemed staged, devoid of any personal belongings. I also noticed an IKEA lamp that didn't seem to fit his persona. For the record, there's nothing wrong with IKEA—I'm a Swede, I love IKEA! Consequently, I do keep track of IKEA inventory. This lamp was one of the cheapest models available. *If he has as much money as he says he does, why wouldn't he spend a little more on a nicer lamp?* I wondered, but I shrugged the purchase off as poor design taste. Continuing our tour, I noticed paperwork conspicuously left out on the kitchen counter that was stamped *LLD Diamonds*.

We then took a trip around town, stopping at places that caught our eye. At one point, we walked past a diamond museum. I love museums, and if I was going to visit a diamond museum, who could be better to accompany me than someone who works in the industry?

"Want to go in here?" I suggested. He agreed it could be fun, and it quickly became apparent that he legitimately knew diamonds. I was impressed by his knowledge as he gave me a guided tour. I had no reason to suspect that he didn't, in fact, work in the industry (I was the one who had suggested going to the museum, after all, so he hadn't staged the visit). My admiration for his expertise, and our overall great rapport, however, didn't translate into romantic chemistry. When he leaned in to kiss me after the tour, I pulled back. "I think we're better off as friends," I said, smiling, and he agreed. We felt more like brother and sister; we'd already established a playful, teasing dynamic.

We made a few other stops before enjoying a pleasant dinner that night, and then relaxed back at his apartment before going to bed.

The next day was more of the same—walking around town, a bit of shopping, and dining out. When we went out to dinner that night, the restaurant staff welcomed him by name and prepared a special order just for him; it was obvious he was a regular. He introduced me quite quickly to people who would confirm his identity. His personal assistant, Joan, who said she'd been working for Simon for years, joined us for the meal. She seemed like a sweet, genuine person. I was relieved by her presence, since Simon and I had determined we were just going to be friends, making our dinner feel less like a date. By the next morning, I was ready to go home but happy with our visit. We enjoyed each other's company and were enthusiastic about becoming travel companions. He told me he was flying to a meeting in South Africa that day, so he had booked a nice car to take us both to the airport. We hugged each other goodbye and agreed to keep in touch.

Over the course of nine months, we built what felt like a close and solid friendship based on our mutual love of travel. We explored Rome together. He joined me on an incredible last-minute trip to Mykonos. To nip any "gold digger" comments in the bud, I always paid for my own flights and hotel rooms after that first initial trip; he would check into the same hotel I was staying in, booking his own room. He would pay our bills at restaurants or treat me to coffee on occasion, but that just felt like polite manners. He was certainly not paying for my holidays.

I didn't realize it at the time, but he was always listening for responses he could mirror back to me, to make himself more likeable. When I gave Simon a hard time for the ostentatious way he dressed, he stopped wearing his flashy watches. When I said I loved history, he booked a historical driving tour through Rome in a Rolls-Royce, which he knew I found classy, and not a Ferrari, which he knew I found flashy.

In the beginning, Simon and I communicated almost every day, throughout each day. He would send me a "good morning" text (he probably had a "good morning" routine with his entire contact list), and we'd have a video call every few days or so. He was always available. If I sent a text saying, "Call me when you have time," he would immediately call me back; he was constantly on his phone. He would casually ask what I was doing and where I was, and he kept track of my socials. I thought he was simply interested in my life, being a caring friend. But he was analyzing my lifestyle, gauging how much money I had. Making sure the relationship, and my trust, was maintained. To Simon, I was a gold mine. He saw that I had money, how I traveled, how I lived, and that I wasn't dependent on a man.

It's ironic now, but Simon made me feel safe. He was the last person on Earth I expected to hurt me.

THE LURE OF SOCIAL MEDIA

One out of ten partnered adults (married, living with a partner, or in a committed romantic relationship) met their significant other through a dating site or app.* Some are fairy-tale stories; others are horror stories.

While romance fraud can occur both online and offline, the overwhelming majority of victims are scouted via dating apps, websites, direct email, or social media platforms.** Communication between the victim and fraudster might remain online or over the phone or move to in-person meetings. Whether online or offline, the nature of the relationship feels deeply intimate, and the victim genuinely feels committed to a partner whom they know well.

Romance scams are nothing new. However, as Maria Konnikova writes in *The Confidence Game*,*** they are remarkably well suited to the modern age. "Cons thrive in times of transition and fast change, when new things are happening and old ways of looking at the world no longer suffice." With the advent of the internet, the world changed in more ways than we could have imagined—and continues

---

* Emily A. Vogels and Colleen McClain, "Key Findings about Online Dating in the U.S.," Pew Research Center, February 2, 2023, https://www.pewresearch.org/short-reads/2023/02/02/key-findings-about-online-dating-in-the-u-s/.

** Cassandra Cross, Molly Dragiewicz, and Kelly Richards, "Understanding Romance Fraud: Insights from Domestic Violence Research," *British Journal of Criminology* 58 (November 2018): 1303–1322, https://academic.oup.com/bjc/article-abstract/58/6/1303/4935144.

*** Marie Konnikova, *The Confidence Game: Why We Fall for It . . . Every Time* (Penguin Books, 2017), 9.

to change seemingly every day. We can now shop, conduct business, plan vacations, and communicate with and meet new people online, including future life partners. It's a landscape we are still learning to navigate. What has become clear is that technology doesn't necessarily make us more knowledgeable, and it certainly doesn't protect us.

In a 2022 report by the FTC, 40 percent of people who lost money to a romance scam said the contact started on social media; 19 percent said it started on a website or app (29 percent named Instagram and 28 percent named Facebook). Reports of romance scams that start with unexpected private messages on social media platforms are most common.

The report also showed that scammers who convince their victims to share explicit photos may then threaten to share them with their victims' social media contacts. This crime—which can accompany romance fraud—is called sextortion and has increased more than eightfold since 2019, with eighteen- to twenty-nine-year-olds over six times as likely to report being victims as people age thirty and over. About 58 percent of sextortion reports in 2022 identified social media as the contact method, with Instagram and Snapchat topping the list.*

IDENTIFYING AND APPEALING TO TARGETS

Romance or relationship fraudsters are basically part-time psychoanalysts, closely monitoring their targets' wants, needs, desires, and insecurities to prey on them. Their first step is identifying the victim: Who are they? What do they want? Then their question becomes, How can I present myself as the perfect vehicle for delivering on those desires?

---

* U.S. Federal Trade Commission, Data Spotlight, "Romance Scammers' Favorite Lies Exposed," February 9, 2023, https://www.ftc.gov/news-events/data-visualizations/data-spotlight/2023/02/romance-scammers-favorite-lies-exposed#ft5.

"One of their greatest skills . . . is to discern details of a victim's life without her knowledge, so that she doesn't even realize how much she's given away, and then use those details to impress the victim with their insight. That ability is the first step of the con . . . the moment when a con artist investigates and chooses his prey. Size someone up well and you can sell them anything,"* Konnikova writes.

While Simon didn't know us before our first dates, he had plenty of information to work with from our Tinder profiles—what we enjoyed, what our lifestyles and financial situations were like, our aspirations, our jobs. Whatever he didn't glean from our profiles, he learned over just a few dates or visits by asking us questions. A quality we were attracted to in him, as both a friend and a romantic partner, was his ability to listen (what woman doesn't want a man who can listen?).

Scammers pay close attention to the information you share, even in passing, so that they can become your perfect match. Once they have a good understanding of what you want, they present themselves as the answer to what you want. You like something, so do they. You're looking to settle down and start a family, they're ready too. They speak in terms of your interests, and by doing so become better liked by and more interesting to you. What makes romance fraudsters so believable? A carefully concocted mixture of belief soup. They create compelling online personas for the person(s) they've identified as their target. "The internet has made establishing a trustworthy identity far simpler than it ever has been. All you need to do is create a firm social media presence, the more accounts the better . . . create a few feeder accounts under other names that seem to support your exclusive affiliations and your value rises even further," Konnikova writes. Some even create fake Wikipedia entries (that stay up long enough for victims to chance upon them) to help boost credentials.**

In some ways, we do a lot of the work for the fraudster; as humans, we are hardwired to believe. Konnikova writes, "We are so bad at

---

* Konnikova, *The Confidence Game*, 57.
** Konnikova, *The Confidence Game*, 155.

spotting deception because it's better for us to be more trusting. We have to be . . . as infants, we need to trust others to meet our needs and desires until we can do it ourselves."* This assumption that—for the most part—people can be trusted creates near perfect conditions for a con artist to thrive. It's also very human to want to love and be loved. Our innate empathy and desire for connection fuels the fraudster's game. Konnikova states that "given the right cues, we're willing to go along with just about anything and put our confidence in just about anyone."**

LOSS OF SOCIAL SUPPORT

Once a "match" on a dating app or connection is made, fraudsters quickly suggest moving the conversation to WhatsApp, Google Chat, or Telegram. According to a 2018 report in the *British Journal of Criminology* titled "Understanding Romance fraud: Insights from Domestic Violence Research,"*** this strategy serves dual purposes: "First, to make the victim feel special, as the move to private communication is often couched in terms of the relationship becoming more serious or 'exclusive.' Second, it minimizes the chance that the offender will be reported to a dating application, website or social media platform as a fraud since communication rapidly moves away from the site." Since many dating websites and apps have strict policies about asking for money directly through their platform, scammers would likely be blocked and/or removed. This strategy is designed to establish trust with the victim, while preventing reporting and increasing isolation.

Not only do offenders attempt to move victims over to private communication channels very quickly, but they often also encourage

---

* Konnikova, *The Confidence Game*, 41.
** Konnikova, *The Confidence Game*, 6.
*** U.S. Federal Trade Commission, Data Spotlight, "Romance Scammers' Favorite Lies Exposed," February 9, 2023, https://www.ftc.gov/news-events/data-visualizations/data-spotlight/2023/02/romance-scammers-favorite-lies-exposed#ft2.

victims not to disclose their new relationship to others, contributing to the victim's sense of isolation. This is a commonly used tactic in both domestic abuse and fraud. Isolation in this context refers to techniques used by the perpetrator to restrict a victim's social networks and activities, making the victim more dependent on the perpetrator. They might monitor their victim's activities (including social media accounts), insist that the victim account for their time, and weaken the victim's support system by restricting their access to communication, thereby limiting their contact with family and friends and support resources. Friends and family, through these restrictions, aren't there to offer "reality checks" to the victim.

Fraudsters often seek not only to isolate their victims from their support networks but to monopolize their victim's time and attention. This behavior is intended to make the abuser the psychological center of the victim's reality and is played out by engaging in continuous—and often interruptive—communication. They may make constant phone calls to victims at home or at work or send frequent texts with the expectation that the victim quickly respond. In abusive situations, the offender's interests always come first. In both romance fraud and domestic abuse situations, possessiveness and jealousy are often used to control victims; fear of displeasing the abuser causes the victim to avoid certain behaviors (such as engaging with others outside the relationship or seeking help).

Since relationship fraudsters often operate from different time zones than their victims—or are constantly on the move—they often engage in late-night communication, which also deprives their victim of the sleep necessary to make rational decisions. Domestic abuse offenders use the same tactic; according to the *British Journal of Criminology* report, "mental exhaustion can decrease resistance to demands, impair victims' thinking and have long-term effects on health and well-being."

Criminologist Dr. Elisabeth Carter adds, "Fraudsters get you used to having very frequent, back-and-forth communication so that when they go silent, you wonder, 'Where are they? Are they all right?' and then you feel relieved when they message you. They are training the victim to be very responsive and to feel like they have to be there for them." Romance fraud is such a perfect opportunity for this crime, because having someone want to communicate frequently with you can feel romantic; someone needs you, and you need them. "For the victim, the feeling of love and all the emotions associated with it are real; there's no way to distinguish truth from falsehoods, because those feelings are chemical reactions." Carter explains that it's a very subtle, gradual transition from needing the victim to be responsive to needing the victim to send them money; money is an extension of their needing you—their vulnerability. "The abuser's willingness to show their vulnerability dulls the victim's alarm bells that something might be off, and makes the victim want to help them. And that's key to the success of this scam—you *want* to help them."

What makes a con artist so believable isn't anything spectacular at all. It's that they seem normal. They're exactly the person you want in your life—attentive, charming, thoughtful, funny. Most likely, they mirror those you're already surrounding yourself with because they've studiously picked up on what you like and don't like. Creepy, we know. Your experience of them seems so completely normal, everything you'd expect to find when you're meeting someone new and building trust with them. And you know they've taken the time to make sure their digital footprint covers their tracks. But that's not all they do to convince you they are who they say they are.

Fraudsters may want *you* to be alone, but they don't act alone. They take their fake identities and false schemes a step further by repeating them with accomplices who validate everything that they're saying.

HOT TIPS

Look for these common signs that a person may be setting you up or grooming you for a scam:

- Unexpected private messages on social media platforms
- Quickly moving communication off dating apps and onto private channels, such as WhatsApp

- Offering deep expressions of love upon first meeting or spontaneous travel invitations, which forces you to make quick decisions with major risks
- Asking too many questions and mirroring your responses
- Asking for personal information, such as your passport details, or explicit photos
- Monopolization of your time with constant communication
- Sleep deprivation (via initiating contact during late hours)

CHAPTER 3

Social Proof: Meet the Accomplices

> ~~Why didn't you verify that he was who he said he was?~~
> How was he able to convince you he was telling the truth?

The golden rule of dating is that you can't really trust a guy until you've met his friends. Well, we both met Simon's colleagues, his good friends, and even his exes. So we might need to throw that rule out.

A scammer can easily create a series of online profiles to create a world that is easily believable to their victims. But it's another thing entirely to have real people playing their part in a fake world convincing you of something. Simon had an entire entourage, a supporting cast that added to his credibility. We (and other victims of Simon's whom we've been in contact with) were introduced to his business partner, Avishay; his bodyguard, Piotr; and other personal assistants, drivers, and friends, as well as hotel staff and airport staff, who all treated him as part of the financial elite. We had no reason to doubt he was who he said he was—the son of a diamond billionaire.

Cecilie

After I agreed to an impromptu flight to Sofia, Bulgaria, on Simon's private jet (I know, it sounds inconceivable to me now), we left the calm, cozy, romantic setting of the hotel café and entered the lobby. A very large, tattooed man who appeared to be of Eastern European descent was introduced to me as Piotr, Simon's bodyguard. A tall blond woman, who looked natural—a bit like me, but older—held her dark-haired, adorable little girl, who was Simon's daughter. I could see that she was her father's child. Then there was a personal assistant named Lindy and three drivers, all awaiting Simon's orders.

There were discussions about what to do and when, who was going to Bulgaria and who was staying in London, and it was Simon calling the shots. Simon became angry because his business partner, Avishay, was supposed to have been there, but he was still lying in his hotel bed, hungover from partying the night before. I felt bad for Simon; I know how it feels to be the responsible one who's always there, fixing things, when someone else doesn't seem to care. I already wanted to help him and be the kind of person he could depend on.

Simon needed to go upstairs and collect his luggage. "Would you like to come with me?" he asked. Of course I did. As we rode the elevator up, just the two of us, he pulled me toward him and gave me a gentle kiss on the lips. I was giddy; I love physical touch, and the tension between us had been building during our coffee date. He had such a magnetic energy around him, I felt so lucky to be the object of his affection.

When we got to his hotel room, I seized on the opportunity to ask him something I'd been wondering. "So, why do you need a bodyguard?"

"Oh, I hired Piotr after I got some threats from competitors. But there's nothing to worry about. He and the security team in Israel are on top of everything." So far, everything I'd experienced had been out of the ordinary, so when Simon was so calm about the security threats, I focused more on how "normal" he made things sound, rather than the uncommonness of the entire situation.

When we got back down to the lobby, Simon walked me outside to where two Rolls-Royces were waiting. He approached one of the cars, which was a convertible, and told the driver, "Can you drive Cecilie to her home so she can pick up her passport and some luggage?" Simon was going to Selfridges, a luxury department store, in a different car with his daughter and her mother, because he wanted to buy his daughter some presents. They would all meet up with me again afterward for lunch before heading to the airport. I said goodbye to Simon and got inside the vehicle. I couldn't believe I was being whisked around London in such a manner!

The driver was very friendly. I told him I had never been in this situation before—luxury cars, private planes—and was feeling a bit overwhelmed. He comforted me by telling me he was Simon's regular driver in London as well as in Amsterdam and said very positive things about Simon. "He's the nicest boss. He always invites me and the other drivers to dinner when we're out." *That's so sweet*, I thought. I respect people who are nice to their staff; I feel it says a lot about a person. My trust in Simon grew.

We arrived at my flat and I went inside to pack. I've never packed so fast in my life! Then Simon's driver took me back to Central London, to where Simon, Piotr, Lindy, and Simon's daughter and her mother and I were all meeting for lunch—a fancy place at the top of Selfridges with opulent décor, pale green walls with gold adornments. A perfect background for lunch with a blended group. The driver even used a lint roller on me before I went inside, so I looked "presentable"! It felt a bit weird but strangely nice. During lunch, I took sneaky photos and texted them to my friends. Neither they nor I could believe the situation I was in.

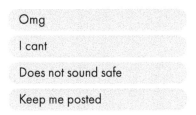

I also couldn't believe how many gifts Simon had bought for his daughter! *What a lucky girl*, I thought. The conversation over lunch felt normal, relaxed.

After lunch, we headed to Farnborough Airport, a business airport forty miles southwest of Central London. Simon and I rode in one of the convertibles, holding hands en route. It was loud with the roof down, so we weren't able to talk much. When we got to the airport, I realized not everyone was going to be on the plane. I had been going with the flow, not asking questions, which I think is what he wanted me to do. My compliance was subtly being tested. Piotr stayed behind, as did Lindy. His daughter and her mother would be coming with us, however. Having his business partner, Avishay, on the flight gave me confidence that the two were going to a business meeting in Sofia. All of us had to be added to the flight paperwork as passengers, which took quite a while. At one point, Simon briefly handed me everyone's passport to hold on to. It was just a split second, but the gesture was strategic. Reflecting back on it, I believe he was checking my level of trust. Would I open them? I didn't. Had I looked, I would have seen that he was using a fake passport.

Shortly into the flight, a white tablecloth was placed on the table I shared with Simon—curtailing my futile attempts to work on my master's thesis—and we were offered champagne, caviar, and sushi. Simon, who had been sitting across from me, got up and moved by my side. My heart fluttered.

Behind us, on a couch, was his daughter's mother. That could have been awkward, but it wasn't . . . probably because Simon had lied to me and said they'd never been in a relationship. For her part, she mostly stayed quiet. I was dying to get some time alone with her. I was so curious to hear what her experience with this man was like . . . girl code, right?

When Simon brought out his camera and started filming us together, I leaned over and gave him a quick kiss on the cheek. After dinner, he wanted to spend time with his daughter. I felt that was endearing; I liked his fatherly side. Our time together on the plane didn't feel like a date; it just felt like I had the privilege of being allowed to spend time with a very busy man, and to see how he interacted with others in both a casual and business setting. Yet the chemistry between us felt undeniable. I loved being around him; something felt really special about him. I didn't want our time together to end.

We didn't arrive in Sofia until around 11 p.m. local time, which was two hours ahead of London. I was so exhausted from processing everything that had happened that day. *How did this become my life?* I thought. All the while, I'd continued updating my friends via text, sending them covert videos I'd taken from the plane. "What are you doing, Cecilie? They could kidnap you!" was their response. It sounds silly to admit, but I hadn't even thought about that. I was so swept up in the moment. One friend was concerned about Simon simply because of the industry he worked in. "You don't become a billionaire being nice," she warned. I brushed their concerns aside. I felt safe with him . . . as did so many other people I'd met that day.

When riding to the hotel in Sofia, I was in a separate car from Simon. I was (finally!) alone with the mother of his daughter. She told me Simon was a great father, he provided for his daughter, and she was happy they were spending time together. When I spoke to her of my impulsive decision to fly to Bulgaria with someone I just met, her calm demeanor made me feel like I was safe.

We checked into the hotel; Simon and I were to share a room, Avishay had his own, and Simon's daughter and her mother had another room. I was so excited to be alone with Simon, at last! The chemistry built, and we made love. Lying in bed, he began to open up to me about his past. I had noticed markings on his back; it looked like he had been beaten or whipped. He told me his previous job was in the weapons industry. A business partner had turned against him and left Simon with the blame for something his partner had done, and Simon ended up in prison in South Africa. He added that, because he was a Jew, he was abused in jail. Cue my "let me start saving you" gene.

"You need proper support in your life," I told him, and of course, I figured that support could be me.

The next morning, Simon had me flown back to London on a commercial flight; he was continuing on to Barcelona for an important business meeting. At the airport, I called my mom. She's a bit like me: a go-with-the-flow person. She felt my excitement for the experience I'd just had and was grateful I was safe and on my way home.

"I don't know if I'll see him again," I told her. "This guy is too busy for a relationship, he has so much going on."

Back at home, however, communication picked up. Simon wrote me every morning and every evening and called me periodically via FaceTime. He sent videos of his hotel rooms and the meals he'd have out. He sent pictures of his daughter; he was bringing me into his life, showing me that he trusted me. I'd get butterflies every time his name popped up on my phone, which I'd entered as *Simon* with a heart emoji. *He really likes me*, I thought, amazed. *I can't believe this is happening to me!*

I thought about him constantly. There was something about his vulnerability that I was drawn to. He was the CEO of a large company, with so many demands placed upon him by so many people. He'd told me that all that responsibility felt heavy. I wanted to protect him, support him.

A week after our trip to Bulgaria, he told me he was coming back to London. I couldn't wait to see him again! Naturally, I wanted to be alone with him, but he already had plans to go out with Avishay and Piotr and invited me along. We ended up at Tramp, a private, members-only club.

Piotr, for his part, stayed in the background, but it seemed like Avishay was always right there, next to us. He was quiet and kept to himself, but it was like having a third wheel on our date. It bothered me that he seemed to take advantage of Simon, leaving most of the work to be done by him. "Why do you let him get away with that?" I asked. "He can't put all the responsibility and pressure on you." Simon told me that Avishay was his old friend who had always been there for him.

"When I was in jail in South Africa, he was the only one who kept in contact with me." Simon showed me pictures of the two of them together as children, which reinforced the belief that Simon was a good person who built long-term, trusting relationships. *I guess I can't argue with that*, I thought, reluctantly.

Simon and Avishay talked business in front of me: what they were going to buy, what they were going to sell. Sometimes their conversations were in English, sometimes they were in Hebrew. As annoying as it was to have Avishay around, he made Simon seem more credible, as a friend and businessperson. I trusted Simon more because of him (which was the whole point).

After Tramp, we went to a casino briefly before going back to his hotel, but we were so tired we didn't have much time awake together. The next morning, he left early to travel. It would be the last time we'd meet up in London. Just after that visit, the "threats" he'd casually told me about when we first met had gotten more serious. "It's not safe for me to come to London right now," he said. I was devastated and scared for his safety, but he kept assuring me that it was temporary, and his security team was handling everything appropriately.

Instead, we made plans to meet briefly in Oslo the following month when I was there for a work seminar (more on that later), followed by Amsterdam, where he was living, and where I met another one of his accomplices. During the visit to Amsterdam, after I'd settled in and was catching up with Simon on the couch in his flat, there was a knock on the door and a woman's voice coming up the stairs.

"Simon! I've got food for you!" Clearly, this person was comfortable enough to let herself in. I stopped midconversation and looked over to Simon, who seemed unfazed.

"Oh, that's just my good friend Joan," he said (the same "Joan" Pernilla met during her first visit with Simon in Amsterdam, only she was introduced to her as Simon's employee). Joan apparently knew he didn't feel well, so she brought over everything to make a home-cooked healthy dinner. As Joan started cooking in the big open kitchen while I sat with Simon at the table nearby, she talked openly about the stress Simon was under, and she seemed especially concerned about the pressures of his businesses. It was clear by Joan and Simon's interactions and her intimate knowledge of his life that they'd been good friends for some time.

I tried to play it cool through dinner and to be warm to Simon's friend, but this whole situation sort of sucked. I'd traveled all the way from London so we could have some quality time together. Besides, Joan was doing all the things I wanted to do to care for him—I wanted to be cooking his meal! I pulled him aside and expressed my discomfort. "Joan is nice, but why did you let her barge in on our date?" I asked. He reassured me about how special I was to him, which helped me get past my doubts (which, okay, were laced with a wee bit of jealousy). Joan's visit reaffirmed that Simon was a good person. This random drop-in by a friend with a home-cooked meal was a sign that he'd built strong friendships with good humans who cared for his well-being. That's the type of guy, someone with a foundation and community, that I was looking for and who Simon claimed to be.

Pernilla

The very first time I met with Simon, he said, "Normally, I have a bodyguard with me."

"Why do you have a bodyguard?" I asked.

"Safety is very important to me," he replied.

I couldn't resist teasing him. "It doesn't sound like it was that important in Thailand." He had just told me about a one-night stand he'd had with a woman there, which had resulted in the birth of his daughter. (He even invited me to FaceTime with his daughter and her mother during that visit; she spoke kindly of Simon and the two of them seemed to have a pleasant rapport. That's some strategy for verifying character!) He looked at me, surprised by my boldness, and we laughed together.

My impression from the beginning was that Simon probably had a bodyguard to look cool, rather than to ward off actual threats. Otherwise, why would he even tell me that he had one? That impression felt further validated when I met Piotr ten days later, when Simon came to visit me in Stockholm. Piotr was Eastern European, tattooed, six and a half feet tall, about two hundred pounds, and always right alongside Simon. *If he were really for security, he would stay more in the background, ready if something were to happen*, I thought.

On that day, something did happen, although I didn't take it seriously. It was Easter weekend. Simon, Piotr, and I were heading out on the town when Piotr came up to Simon and said, "There is a security issue. Someone hacked the system." Simon appeared stressed. He showed me some strange email messages he'd received and clearly expected a reaction from me that I did not give him.

"I get strange messages all the time," I said, brushing his concern off. They dropped the subject, and I didn't give it any further thought or energy. We enjoyed the rest of our visit together and then parted ways.

About a week later, I received a voice message from Simon. "Someone tried to stab me," he said. He told me he'd been out with Piotr in Copenhagen when "his competitors" attacked him. The message was accompanied by photos of a cut on Piotr's head, Simon with Piotr's blood on his shirt, and videos of them riding in an ambulance. They were headed to the hospital to get Piotr stitched up. Once again, I didn't give him the reaction he'd expected.

"Oh, come on, you got into a bar fight and Piotr had to protect you. Admit it," I teased. I'd seen how Simon could get quite cocky when out drinking, and I assumed he'd triggered someone else who was drunk; maybe he'd been flirting with his woman or something. He then mirrored my story.

"Yes, you're right, someone threw a bottle at me, and Piotr stepped in front of it."

I gave him a friendly warning. "You have to behave when you're out drinking, Simon. Take care of yourself."

"I know, I'll be more careful," he promised.

I never did see Piotr again; he wasn't there on my subsequent visit to Amsterdam, which was a trip I'd already had planned with my grandparents and my cousin to see the tulip fields. Simon was there with another cast of characters, however.

Simon's meeting place of choice was the Conservatorium, a luxury hotel in the Museum Quarter that was near his apartment. We made plans to meet there for coffee, just the two of us. He greeted me outside when I arrived, and as we walked in, the doorman, bellmen, and front desk staff all said the same thing: "Welcome back, Mr. Leviev." He was known there. We got comfortable and ordered drinks in the Lounge, a light-flooded atrium in the center of the hotel. The Lounge was like a giant living room, perfect for hosting not just me but the other women Simon would bring along or ask to stop by.

I met up with him three times during that trip; the list of his guests coming and going included Simon's personal assistant, Lindy, who'd worked for Simon for a few years. She was a super smart young woman whom I liked right away. Later, Joan stopped in briefly; I had met her on my first visit to Amsterdam, and she had also said she'd been working for Simon's company for years. She brought along some girls for Simon to meet while out for drinks the second night, and then at lunch the next day, Simon had a new date with him. Having other women there made me drop my guard a bit. The fact that he had these intelligent, kind women working for him and dating him made me feel safer and certain that he could be trusted . . . because otherwise they would let me know, right?

There were no red flags, security threats mentioned, or seemingly any cause for concern. I did think he was a very intense dater; he always seemed to have a different woman by his side! I thought it was a bit much, but I shrugged it off as his being young and wanting to have fun.

Sometimes we hung out at Simon's apartment during my visits to Amsterdam. He'd occasionally say, "Hold on, I'm getting a business call," then step into the bedroom, but not close the door, and have the phone on speaker. In retrospect, it was as if I were not supposed to hear but was also supposed to hear. He'd then tell me he'd been talking to his business partner, Avishay (whom I wouldn't meet in person until after I learned I was being defrauded).

After that second visit to Amsterdam, I had a trip booked to Mykonos, Greece, in July with one of my best friends. Simon thought it sounded like a good time and asked if he could meet up with us there. I told him that sounded great and gave him the dates we'd be there and the hotel we were staying at. He booked a jet and a room at the hotel and stayed there for two nights. He brought along his new girlfriend, Polina, and the four of us had a great time going out for meals and hanging out on the beaches. Simon was particularly busy during that time, though, and often on his phone.

"What's going on?" I asked him, wondering why he couldn't just put the phone down and relax.

"There's a lot of stress with work. There are some problems I have to take care of," he said, but didn't go into any detail.

A month later, he invited me to meet up with him and Polina in Rome, Italy. He knew I'd never been there and insisted I'd love the city because I love history—especially gladiators. "Come join us, it will be fun," he said. "We'll be staying at the Waldorf Astoria." He gave me all the details of his trip, and I booked my flight and my own room at the same hotel. That was the trip where he really put on a show—not just for me, but for his girlfriend, Polina. Cecilie and I call his fraud tactics "immersive theater," and boy could he (and his accomplices) put on a performance.

I arrived at the hotel on the evening of August 24 and immediately started getting ready to go out for dinner. Simon and Polina came to pick me up in a Rolls-Royce. We enjoyed a nice meal out, then were driven around to some of the popular tourist sites. Simon had planned everything out—a private sightseeing tour of sorts that extended into the next two days, visiting historical sites that he knew would interest me. That first night, we visited the Trevi Fountain. I have video of myself throwing coins into the fountain, saying, "Wish me luck!" *This is going to be the best year of my life!* I thought, a broad smile on my face. If only I had known. We visited a couple more sites that night, then went back to the hotel to sleep.

The next day, we went to the Colosseum, but this time, a woman named Claudia joined us. Claudia introduced herself as Simon's tech safety assistant and said she had been working for LLD Diamonds for several years, before transitioning to full time with Simon three years ago (all of which were verified on her LinkedIn profile). Simon referred to her as an IT expert. "She could hack the hotel's system," he bragged. She spoke openly about the Leviev family and the company history, which Simon encouraged. He'd interrupt, "Tell her about the time . . ." or "Tell her about that other time . . ." She gave a full-on performance.

"His brother is great, but his sister is a bit difficult," she said, followed by stories about each of them. She seemed to have intimate knowledge about Simon, his family, and other employees. While we women shopped, Simon was off talking on the phone, which continued well after we were ready to leave. We sat in the car, waiting for him to end his call outside. "He does this all the time," Claudia said. "He's been so busy with work."

The trip came to a close. Simon and I stayed in regular contact by phone but didn't see each other over the next couple of months. I was busy with my own life, which involved a lot of travel that year. I never saw Polina or Claudia again.

There was so much going on in Simon's scheme, all at once: small stories that built and built until the fraud finally started in November 2018—nine months after we'd first met. By then, however, there had been simply too many data points, externally validated by a variety of seemingly normal people, that lined up perfectly. Consciously and subconsciously, all these ancillary relationships verified details, confirmed Simon's false identity, and gave him the perfect cover of a totally normal, charming, trustworthy guy.

RINSE AND REPEAT

"One of the strongest motivators in our being persuaded [by scammers] is we are more likely to go along with something if it has the stamp of approval of a group we trust,"* Maria Konnikova wrote. Simon's identity became more and more true to us the more we were around him. The accomplices played a role in that, as did our daily conversations that reiterated who he was and what he was going through. A con artist will use repetition in all its forms, including

---

* Konnikova, *The Confidence Game*, 259.

social proof, in order to engender trust. You'll have no reason not to believe them.

According to Lisa Fazio, researcher and assistant professor of psychology at Vanderbilt University, if we hear false information repeated, we're more likely to believe it to be true. It's known as the *illusory truth effect* and works even when we have prior knowledge of the truth or the information contradicts what we'd normally think or what we already know.

The fraudster's web is established through what criminologist Dr. Elisabeth Carter refers to as the "setup and drip feed." She told us in an interview, "The 'setup and drip feed' is the term I coined to describe the perpetrator's tactics of setting out 'facts' that are used to explain or contextualize requests for money later on in the relationship, so they don't appear 'out of the blue.' For example, early on in the relationship, the perpetrator will deliver information on their own values and their hopes for a future partner. This will often include attributes such as generous, loyal, willing to take a chance on love, supportive, and trusting, which are all acceptable and not unusual relationship requirements. Once agreed, these are then used to make the victim later feel as though if they do not assist by giving money, they are not living up to their agreed relationship."

In this way, information is shared early on with the victim and is then repeated, developed, and relied on to validate future behaviors and requests. Carter said, "Fraudsters don't necessarily use certain words and phrases, but the essence is always the same. They first establish credibility and rapport; there are a few ways they do this, including making themselves look a bit vulnerable. If they're on a dating site, they might say they are new to the dating site or haven't dated for a while. This makes them look nonthreatening and makes the victim feel protective: 'Don't worry, I am new to this as well, we'll discover it together.'" The playing field is leveled, she explained, rather than one person being more powerful. "The fraudster will offer a lot of information than they normally would in a romantic relationship, which is why it's so powerful a crime, because you exchange information that you wouldn't normally give to other people. Revealing details about themselves establishes trust. Those details are all fake, we realize later, but they all seem reasonable at the time."

There will be talk of money and business, but there will be no request for money for quite a while. "They might subtly mention cash flow difficulties, such as 'Business is great, but I've got to set some money aside for issues coming up later. But it's nothing for you to worry about.' Of course, it will become something for you to worry about later on but they park that information, so when they do 'need' money, the victim will think, 'Oh, yeah, you talked about that earlier.'"

In preparation for the eventual "ask," fraudsters will test your level of compliance. Carter says, "If they can get you to comply with small asks with very little stakes, they will know it's worth investing in a relationship with this person. These small asks will groom the victim into a position where doing something they ask for is normal. Psychologically, if you've already said yes to something, even if it has nothing to do with money, you're likely to say yes to something else in the future, even if it's outside your comfort zone." Which is why when a romance scammer tells the victim they're sick, hurt, or in jail (or another fake reason that requires the victim to send them money), the victim often doesn't hesitate. They love this person. They trust this person. They want to protect this person.

By the time something "unfortunate" happens and the fraudster needs money, the victim feels they are in control of their position to help; even when everything becomes out of control later on, they still feel in control, because the asks are incremental. "You don't notice how crazy it becomes, because each ask links to what happened previously, and is always for just a little bit more, or just one more time."

The fraudster's strategy is designed to disincentivize questioning what they say, because in the victim's mind, doing so would mean they were being untrustworthy or unserious about the relationship. The victim also gets to a point where they don't feel they can tell anyone about what is going on, because even though they "know" what's going on is real, they know it would sound crazy to other people. They feel they're on their own at that point and just have to keep going. Without the support of a trusted social network to cross-check their gut feelings, the victim is instead encouraged to take the fraudster's word as the truth. Simon's word, after all, had been validated many times over by others he'd introduced us to.

Many of the people making these events possible for Simon would come back full circle. After we exposed Simon for his crimes, we found a Facebook group called Victims of Shimon Hayut (aka Simon Leviev). As we scrolled through the members list, a few faces and names looked wildly familiar. Many of the people we'd met who had confirmed Simon's identity and his business were in this group. They posted messages about the money Simon had taken from them and never repaid. Each of them offered a compelling story, similar to ours.

So why then had they gone on to help him defraud us? If they had gone through the same pain and emotional abuse that we had, how could they let him do that to someone else? Maybe they hadn't realized at the time that they were being defrauded (and so were we). Or, if they had, maybe the old saying is true: *Hurt people hurt people.*

Clearly, they were benefiting in some way. Likely, they were told that they could get their money back if they did what he asked them to. People who have lost it all become desperate to regain at least some of what they lost, to be able to move on with their lives. The lies and the hurt, therefore, got perpetuated further and further.

In textbook examples, scams that hinge on co-conspirators use people who have been conned themselves and become accomplices because they're told they'll profit. That's exactly what we think happened with Joan, Claudia, and Simon's ex who was the mother of his daughter (Simon went to prison in Finland in 2015, under his real name of Shimon Hayut, for conning her). That doesn't make any of them innocent. When Cecilie contacted Joan through Messenger after she discovered that Simon was a fraudster, she didn't receive a reply, but we know she went straight to Simon. When Pernilla contacted Joan after she learned about Simon, Joan claimed she hadn't known he was a fraudster but sent Simon the police report Pernilla had sent her. Lindy had been dating Simon at one time, but Simon told us that she was only an assistant. We got to know later that she was a victim as well, and she had to flee to another country.

Although Pernilla only met Claudia, Simon's alleged tech safety assistant, once, she was a major accomplice in her story. When Pernilla was waiting on a transfer from Simon to repay her loan, he sent Pernilla voice messages he had received from Claudia—for example, "I have spoken to the bank and they just needed some more documents, so I sent those in, and it shouldn't be more than two or three days before Pernilla receives the money. Oh, and regarding David, he's looking for a (particular type of) diamond, so if you could get back to me with that, that would be great." Former victim or not, she knew what she was doing.

We don't know if Piotr and Avishay were former victims, but they certainly had skin in the game. Avishay was always more in the background, never really giving much away about his personal life. What we do know is there's no way he didn't know that Simon wasn't really Simon Leviev; one key bit of evidence we would find out during the course of our research is that when Simon was arrested as Shimon Hayut in Israel, Avishay paid his bail. We've seen childhood photos of the two of them together, so their relationship goes way back. We also know that Simon paid for Avishay's flights, with victims' credit cards. Whether he knew that was how Simon was paying for the flights we can't say for certain, but he was definitely enjoying the fruits of Simon's crimes and playing a fake role, right along with Simon. Video from when Cecilie was on the private jet with Simon and Avishay shows them both wearing the same outfit, joking with the stewardess that they work for the same company.

When we connected all these dots, we knew we'd never file a civil lawsuit in order to try to recoup some of our money. The only money Simon had—or would have in the future—was money from other victims. It was blood money.

HOT TIPS

- The existence of "friends" online or in real life shouldn't be enough to let your guard down—fraudsters rarely act alone.

- Be aware of the "setup and drip feed"—information shared early on that is repeated, developed, and relied on to validate future behaviors and requests, such as making themselves appear vulnerable or dropping comments about possible threats or risks "that you don't need to worry about." Accomplices may be used to validate these risks.

- Cross-check your gut feelings with your own supportive network, not someone else's—and especially not the fraudster's.

CHAPTER 4

Emotional Grooming

~~How could you be so stupid as to give him so much money?~~
What were the strategies he used to manipulate you?

An emotional foundation must be laid before any scheme is proposed. Victims of relationship fraud aren't simply asked to send money to the scammer; they are manipulated and groomed over time into an emotional state that makes them more susceptible to agreeing to the request. As Maria Konnikova explains, "Someone who is emotional is someone who is vulnerable. And so . . . before a single persuasive appeal is made . . . the emotional channels are opened. (And) in that first rush of romantic infatuation, we abandon our reason."*

Just looking for love makes us vulnerable. We're opening our heart, inner thoughts, and personal history to someone new, trusting them to keep us safe . . . making dating apps the perfect platform for exploitation. Romance fraudsters get us to imagine a promising future together; they speak of marriage, starting a family, and anything else they know we want because we told them, and they've been listening and mirroring our desires back to us. They present themselves as the "perfect person," asking all the right questions to gauge us and become the person we've been looking for. Then they start to rope us in.

---

* Konnikova, *The Confidence Game*, 92.

Simon was very good at faking love, whether it be romantic love or friendship love. Now we know that what he was doing is called *love bombing*—overly emotional brainwashing, a tactic used in abusive relationships. He made us feel confident in our relationship, deeply wanted, and the most important person in his life. He made us afraid of losing him. The narrative that romance fraudsters sell is exactly what our generation grew up watching in romantic comedies and Disney movies: girl meets boy, boy immediately sweeps girl off feet, something difficult occurs that threatens to keep them apart (for example, "enemies" are introduced), couple stays strong together, marries, and lives happily ever after.

That's the narrative that Simon used on us.

Cecilie

Simon started love bombing me right from the top, although I didn't recognize it for what it was. For my thirtieth birthday, he sent me one hundred red roses. He flooded me with statements like "You're my dream woman" and "I want to marry you" and "I've never felt like this before. I never could have imagined this, ever" and even "You know me so well without knowing me." Basically, "I heard everything that you told me about what you want from your life, and here it is (and be careful not to lose it)." I felt lucky that he wanted to be with me, and his communication was so consistent that I never questioned his feelings toward me. Now I know that the constant messaging and phone calls were ways to make me a part of his daily life—always top of mind—and make me feel special.

When he video called one day, my mother was visiting me in London and she got on the call with us. "I can't wait to meet you," Simon told her, smiling. "I'm going to make you some Israeli food." My mom was so happy because she could see how happy I was.

"That would be lovely," she said. "You must come to Norway."

"Yes, I will definitely do that," he promised her.

She ended the call with "Take good care of my daughter," and of course, he assured her that he would. If he didn't really care about me, he wouldn't have made the effort to talk to my mother, right?

To drive home the message that he envisioned a future with me in it, he asked me what I thought about us living together in London. My response was, of course I wanted to! Having a stable home life, him coming home from work and us making dinners together, cuddling on the couch, going for walks around the neighborhood, exploring small coffee shops . . . I wanted to do it all. With us together, I felt invincible.

He was certain the security situation would sort itself out, and since he was so busy and traveling so much, he asked me to go apartment hunting for us in London. He told me the budget was $10,000/month. I attended open houses, sending him videos of luxury flats that I could now see myself living in with him. I video called him when I found the perfect flat, and he talked directly to the real estate agent. Afterward, the agent commented that Simon knew what he was talking about and was good at negotiating. Our shared dream felt closer to reality.

Because we'd both been so busy, we made plans to celebrate Valentine's Day together a bit late, when I was in Oslo for a work seminar. When I first suggested the idea of meeting there since he couldn't come to London, he made a point of saying, "Babe, I don't have any business in Oslo. There's nothing for me to do there, other than see you." By carving time out of his crazy schedule and taking a special flight to Oslo to spend one night with me, he was showing me how much I meant to him. I was thrilled.

He was supposed to fly into Oslo at four p.m. on a Sunday, but then he kept texting me, postponing his departure time. "I'm so sorry, I'm caught up with work and will have to leave later, but I promise I will be there." Four in the afternoon became seven in the evening, then eight. I was angry, disappointed, and embarrassed.

"Babe, I feel stupid now because I made plans with my friends here to meet you, and now you're not here."

"Cecilie, I'll be there. I'm a man of my word."

By ten p.m. or so, I put my phone on silent and went to bed. I had work the next morning and was not going to stay up for him. I doubted that he would come at all; he'd have to leave Oslo by the following morning. When I woke up the next morning at five a.m., I was shocked to see a message from him, sent around midnight: "I'm in Oslo," with a link to the hotel he was staying at.

> 00:00 Simon: You up ?
>
> 05:49 Cecilie: I was sleeping babe:(
>
> 06:00 Simon: I'm in Oslo
>
> [Simon has shared his location: Hotel Continental Oslo]
>
> 06:00 Cecilie: Are you??? Awww babe, Im going to get ready quick, and get to you?
>
> 06:01 Simon: Ok call me when you're down, I'm sleeping.. Didn't sleep all night
>
> 06:53 Cecilie: I'm here
>
> 06:54 Simon: Coming down
>
> 07:52 Cecilie: So nice seeing you again. A little sad as well. Because I understand I won't see you in a while again. I hope everything settles down soon. I want you to be able to live in peace
>
> 08:03 Simon: Yes me too honey thank you for the gifts. It was amazing seeing you my honey
>
> 08:24 Cecilie: Ijust want to see you more now. haha
>
> 09:07 Simon: You will I promise

> 09:13 Cecilie: I care about you so much. And its so weird. Im scared of my feelings.
> But it was so good seeing you. Like everything is ok as long as im with you.

> 09:25 Simon: Thanks honey I feel the same baby. I will read your book.

> 11:03 Cecilie: You have to. Your new safe country! haha And read the messages why you're wonderful. Think you need to hear it.

> 11:04 Simon: You are honey thanks for the gift

> 11:07 Cecilie: Just wanted to give something small back.

> 11:08 Simon: I really appreciate everything you doing for me

> 12:21 Cecilie: Im not doing much I feel babe
> ✓✓

He'd landed at the airport in the middle of the night just to spend time with me for a few hours! My disappointment changed to elation. *Wow, he* really *likes me! He* is *a "man of his word."* Maybe his delay was part of the emotional trope: disappoint me, then get me super excited that he actually came. It made me forget all about the fact that I'd been angry. I was always on a roller coaster of emotions with him.

I showered and got dressed, then met up with him at his hotel room. I was so glad to see him! I gave him my Valentine's Day gift—a list of "ten reasons why you're wonderful" and a playful book about what it was like to date a Norwegian. He told me how happy he was to see me, and then told me more about the threats he was getting. He'd been receiving phone calls at hotels he was staying at under a fake name, saying, "We found you." He even showed me photos of items he'd received in the mail—bullets and funeral flowers. Then he showed me security camera footage of his Tel Aviv apartment that had been broken into. I was so terrified for him. Things had escalated since the last time I'd seen him.

"Is there anything I can do to help?"

"It's okay, baby, it's under control. Your support means so much to me, though, I really appreciate it," he said. "But I want to be honest with you that the diamond industry is a dangerous business. If it's too much for you to handle, I understand. You do not have to stay with me."

Hearing that made me want to be with him even more. I wanted to protect him. He knew that would be my reaction.

Then, a day or two later, I received a voice note from Simon.

"I have some problems now. I don't know what to do."

"What's going on. You're safe, right?"

"They've told me I can't use my credit cards anymore, and it's making a lot of trouble."

And then the request came.

"I wanted to ask you a favor. If you have an American Express credit card or something, I can link it to my account. And then it's not under my name so basically nobody knows anything. Of course I will cover everything in advance, but yeah that would be great. Thank you so much, I really appreciate it."

I told him I don't have an American Express card. "You can apply for one," he said. When I look back at it, I didn't have a gut feeling that this was a red flag, or that he was going to scam me. I knew he had a lot of money. When I'd heard about fraudsters before, they were in situations where they needed money. Simon, as I knew him, needed nothing of the kind. I'd experienced his lifestyle, I'd met his friends, co-workers, and business partner. Besides, he hadn't asked for money, directly; he'd asked for a "favor." In hindsight it sounds ridiculous, but the "favor" he was asking me for felt small at the time: the temporary use of a card with my name on it—for two weeks at most, he told me—to protect him from being found by dangerous people. I was scared for him—and for me, because my name was now involved—but the alternative felt much worse. He could be killed, I thought.

"Don't be scared," he wrote. "I promise, you have nothing to worry about. Everything will be fine. One million percent. It's you and me. I trust you, and you have trusted me. Trust me with this matter as well." He continued using collective language: "we" will get through this, "we" are in this together. It was now "us" versus "them"—whoever "they" were.

"Okay. I trust you," I replied. "This is just a difficult situation for the both of us and a dangerous one for you."

Before he ever asked for help, I had already offered, "Is there anything I can do for you?" That was exactly what he wanted me to ask, but his early response was always "No, of course not. That's not your responsibility. Everything is going to be fine." When the money requests came, I was fully primed. I was in love, convinced he was in danger, needed help, was wealthy, and would have no issue paying me back.

When I go back and review my communication with him from those days, it's hard for me to understand how I couldn't see what he was doing. I guess the cliché is true—love is blind. I wanted so badly to believe in the fairy tale. Even my concept of time was warped; I didn't recognize how little time had passed (two months!) between meeting for the first time and talk of moving in together, marriage, and finally, requests for money. He had kept me in an emotionally charged state where time existed outside reality. And because of my naturally trusting nature and how quickly I tend to fall in love, I was easy prey. He could see very early on how much of a romantic I was. I would say things like "I hate how much I miss you" and "I feel so secure with you" and "I trust you." I was writing exactly what he as a fraudster wanted someone to write to him. I was love bombing him!

This is what fraudsters do. They get you to trust them, to feel secure with them. I loved Simon. I loved the aura around him; he was funny and charismatic and enjoyable to be around (which, of course, he used to his advantage). He gave me so much from the emotional aspect as well; when I was feeling down, he would always lift me up. And of course, he gave me new life experiences, which I was grateful for (although they were the very experiences that distracted me from what he really wanted from me). I felt I owed him something for all of that.

After Oslo, our next meetup was in Amsterdam, at the end of February. I had received the American Express card through my UK bank in the mail and had already begun using it for online purchases for Simon, but we made plans for me to deliver the physical card to him in person so that he could use it directly.

"We're going to have to be a team," he said. "The bank will call you every single day to verify that you are the one making the transactions, or else they will block the card. So you have to know where I am and what I've used the card for. Okay?"

"Of course. You can trust me." So much of what Simon was exposing me to was completely new to me. From sitting in a Ferrari and flying on a private jet to having a credit card and (later) cashing a check . . . not having experience or understanding how large bank transfers work or how companies are structured, for example, made it hard for me to feel comfortable asking questions. He knew these things better than me, so I should just trust him, right? Whenever I expressed any doubt about what I was doing, he would reassure me that everything was okay, and I would feel better again. He made me feel special and loved.

> "If I wasn't sure about you, I would never share with you my life, I
> would never have you meet my daughter if you weren't important to me. I would never
> ask you for the Amex, never, never, never. Everything is fine. I care about you. I miss
> you and everything will be alright baby. Thanks for being with me to the bitter end. I
> appreciate it so much. And I'm thinking that life is not supposed to be easy, but I was
> supposed to meet you. I really feel that."
> ▶

Simon's apartment in Amsterdam was in a nice neighborhood close to Vondelpark, on the corner above a restaurant. According to Simon, his family owned the entire building. When I arrived, he led me through a small door and up a narrow staircase that opened to his recently refurbished apartment that he called his "hideaway." It was decorated in a cool, modern way that made it look like he cared about aesthetics, but he wasn't trying hard. I didn't think the place was all that personal, but I shrugged it off. That's true of a lot of rich people's houses.

It was a short visit: just one night. I had to leave early for work the next day. We had just enough time to go for a beautiful walk together around the city and share a nice meal. Over dinner, Simon told me more about what his competitors were up to—the latest threats he'd received, and tactics his security team had implemented to evade them. Then we went back to his apartment to tend to business.

I gave him the AMEX card. "This needs a higher credit limit, baby," he said.

I told him that's the credit limit I was approved for based on my income.

He was prepared for this. "I can just make you an employee at LLD Diamonds."

My logical brain thought, *This doesn't feel right*. But I talked myself into accepting it. He was the CEO of the company, so if he went through the company process to make me an employee, I technically wasn't lying, right? I had no idea how that decision would come back to haunt me.

Simon dialed a number and put the phone on speaker. "Hello, I want to employ Cecilie Fjellhøy," he told a man on the other end.

"Of course, Mr. Leviev," the man replied, and asked for my passport details. Before long, documents were sent over on official company letterhead, along with pay slips to verify my new "income" of $100,000 per month. An absurd number, which should have triggered an alarm with AMEX but didn't seem to. (Whoever forged those documents was a professional; members of the real Leviev family would later be shocked by how authentic they looked.) In the end,

I was able to get $85,000 in credit (an insane amount in only three weeks).

I returned to London, and our communication remained constant throughout March. This wasn't a "take the money and run" situation. Surely, if he was a scammer, once he had the credit card, he would quickly spend the money and ghost me before I had a chance to figure it out, right? But no, he had bigger plans for me. His security situation was consuming him, and consequently me. He'd quickly maxed out my AMEX credit card, even with the increased limit. The first payment was coming due, and I was growing more and more anxious; I knew the repercussions of not paying down the debt.

"Simon, I really need you to send me money to pay down the card," I reminded him.

"Yes, my love, I will make a transfer in just a few days." Then Simon told me he'd made a payment transfer directly to my AMEX account and sent me a screenshot of the transaction. But when I called AMEX to notify them that they'd be getting the direct transfer, they said, "That's going to bounce. We don't take direct transfers from other people's accounts." Simon must have known that, but the attempt offered the illusion that he was trying to make things right.

What happened next is embarrassing to admit; I can see now how naïve I was, but I was so immersed in the story, I couldn't remove the veil from my eyes. And the pressure Simon put me under was immense; I was constantly fielding calls from AMEX, having to approve new purchases. Calls would come in while I was at work, attending meetings and facilitating workshops, putting added stress on me as I tried to keep up with my professional responsibilities when I was already running on little sleep. Interestingly, I wasn't angry at Simon, I was angry at the situation he was in.

"You can take out loans to pay down the AMEX card until I can pay you back another way," Simon suggested. He was in desperate need of money in order to continue conducting business while he was waiting for the security issues to pass. He was working on a critical $73 million deal that was close to going through.

I was so certain that he was a billionaire. Of course he would be able to pay me back! And I wanted to do the "right" thing, as his girlfriend. I wanted to protect him, to keep him safe and happy. Plus, I wanted all of this to be over with, so we could relax and enjoy life together. I would do anything to help get us closer to that point.

I was shocked by how easy it was to take out loans in Norway. I was asked for a few months' pay slips to verify income and sometimes just the previous year's tax return. My credit score was high, so I'm sure that helped. I'd heard stories about people who had gotten into trouble after taking out a high-interest loan; I now saw how the interest piled up so fast and understood how one loan could easily destroy someone's financial life. But not for a moment did I think that could be me. It's hard to explain, but I didn't think I was accruing debt, I was just accepting emergency cash that was going to be paid back before any interest kicked in. I was the girlfriend of a billionaire, and this was an emergency situation. He just needed my help for a bit.

I took out four high-interest loans between March 25 and March 27.

$10,000—Bank Norwegian
$50,000—Instabank
$50,000—Bank Norwegian
$12,500—DNB Finance

Over $122,000 in just a few days, on top of the $85,000 in credit card debt. The debt didn't even scare me. Now I would describe what I felt then as an out-of-body experience; it wasn't me taking out the loans, but Simon and me as a team.

I used the loans to pay down the AMEX card. Then, on March 27, Simon issued a transfer from the company's bank in Hong Kong to my account. He showed me the transfer receipt, in the amount of $250,000. I couldn't believe it! That was far more than he owed me. I'd be able to pay off all the loans I'd taken out, and then some.

While waiting for the Hong Kong transfer to go through (it was a holiday weekend, so I figured it might take longer), AMEX blocked my credit card. They had waited until right after I made a $50,000 payment to block the card. Simon had been right; they did try to verify that I was the one using the card, and in this case they had already come to a conclusion.

"We are contacting you about the use of your card," an AMEX representative called and told me. "We know you are not the one using your card." They did not use the word *fraud* or suggest that I was being scammed. What they said and how they said it sounded accusatory, which immediately put me on the defensive. I became scared that I was going to get in trouble for allowing Simon—my boyfriend—to use my card, which pushed me into Simon's court even more. I leaned toward the one person who said everything was going to be okay.

When you're scared of what's going to happen or about what you have to fix, you're not in the headspace to think clearly. To demonstrate how delusional my mind was at the time—between the stress and the pressure Simon and the entire situation had put me under, the lack of sleep, the emotional manipulation I didn't even know was happening—I had started to believe all the lies I'd been telling myself.

"What are you talking about? Of course I'm the one that's been using the card!" I went so far as to file an email complaint after I got off the phone.

> Hi!
> I just had a chat with your credit review team that wasn't all too pleasant. I suffer from stammering, and how I was approached did not help. I was totally set back.
> From I opened the account Ive had plenty of contact with you. I have been giving you and providing you with all the information you have asked, and not once has it been questioned before.
> Now that I payed down almost the entire balance before due date, you tell me I'm under investigation. And are questioning my credibility, when all Im doing is using the card (aka providing you with more cash) and then paying it

down. I have no idea why you have a problem with the use and spend on the card, when Im actually paying it down before time.
I have no idea why you have decided to block it, but this is also making me question if want to be a customer either if this is the treatment I will receive. Its possible to be nice and not having an accusing tone.
Im awaiting more calls, but it would bee nice to being talked to in a proper way.

- Cecilie Fiellhoy

I was so convinced that I—we—were in the right. *It's Simon and me together. It's us against the world.*

Now without the use of my card, Simon asked for cash. Twenty-five thousand dollars to continue to conduct business, because cash was untraceable. My first thought was *That's not even possible.* A bank would never release that much cash to someone like me, would they? But Simon coached me through it. "Don't worry, I know you can do it. It will work, I promise. We're in a war now. There's no one else."

He was so good at giving me reassurance. And he was right—in a way, there was no one else. I wasn't telling any of my friends or family what I was doing. He got me to be another person who only listened to him.

I was so nervous walking into Lloyds Bank, but I put on my best friendly face.

"Hi, I need twenty-five thousand dollars cash to travel to South Africa with some friends," I told the teller. I wasn't truly aware of my privilege until then. People trust me because of how I look. As a blond, white, female Norwegian living in London, I believe I was seen as squeaky clean. It's interesting, but I trusted Simon in the same way, because of how he looked. He was a man of faith, who showed me his lavish business lifestyle. I didn't feel there was anything to question (and no one else was questioning him, either).

The teller told me there was a withdrawal limit of $6,000 per transaction but offered to place my request as four different transactions, for a total of $24,000. I'd have to come up with another way to get the final $1,000 to stay under the daily limit. I was told I could either have the cash delivered to my home or pick it up from the bank. Rather than walk the streets of London with that amount of cash, I opted to have it delivered to my apartment, which seemed surreal. I felt like I was in a movie. *Well, you asked for an exciting life, Cecilie.*

"I've got the money, babe," I wrote Simon. "I'll need to get another $1,000 from another bank. I hope that's okay?" I actually asked him if that was okay. I wanted so badly to please him: to earn his respect and love and do what he asked me to do, to show him how much I loved him. In retrospect, a part of me must have felt like I might lose him if I couldn't fulfill his wishes . . . or, perhaps, that I wasn't worthy of his love. He still felt larger than life to me. My brainwashed mind justified everything I was doing as necessary for the one I loved. "Your girl is getting things fixed," I said proudly.

"I knew you'd be able to do it!" he replied.

I still had to get the cash to him, though.

"You can bring it to me here," he suggested. "I will book you a flight to Amsterdam." My visit was over Easter weekend, Thursday, March 29 to Monday, April 2. In my head, it was a much-needed visit to physically and emotionally reconnect with my boyfriend, who had been under so much stress. My love-fogged (and exhausted and stress-filled) brain didn't even see what was right in front of me—for him, it was none other than a visit to gain access to more money . . . while he had me thinking he'd already paid me back.

I went through airport security with $25,000 cash in my suitcase. I was nervous, for sure, but Simon had made it seem so simple, so normal. "Nothing bad will happen, my love, no one is going to say anything. It's not like you're a bank robber." Shockingly, he was right. I made it through security without any type of questioning.

I arrived at his apartment in Vondelpark and gave him not only the cash but a new DNB Mastercard.

"Thank you so much, baby, I really appreciate it." I was delighted I'd pleased him. *Now we can relax*, I thought. Only an hour into my visit, however, Simon's bodyguard, Piotr, called. Simon put him on speakerphone.

"They found you, Simon!" Piotr was yelling, panicked. "There's a private jet ready for you. You need to leave now."

"What? Cecilie just arrived, I can't just leave her here," Simon argued. As he spoke, he rushed around the house turning off the lights, double-checking the locks, and pulling down the blinds. Once again, I felt like I was in a movie. *What is happening?* After what felt like hours but was only a minute or two, Simon got off the phone, having finally agreed to leave Amsterdam.

My anxiety was raging, just as he'd expected it to. "What is going on, Simon?"

"My enemies have found me. I need to leave immediately. You can stay here. I will message you after I land." He kissed me goodbye.

"What? What am I supposed to do?" I was crying, terrified of being left alone. Would his enemies come to the apartment? What would they do to me? My logical brain, which would have told me that if Simon really cared about me, he would have ensured my safety before he left, was once again hijacked by fear—not just for my life, but for his.

"Just stay here and keep the doors locked. I will come back after the security situation has cleared." He assured me everything would be okay. And for him, it was. Shortly after he left me alone in his apartment, like within minutes, he wrote to Pernilla and said he was lonely and wanted to come to Stockholm. His voice notes to me after he left told a different story.

"I love you and I miss you. We are strong and we are against everybody. We are in a war now. We just don't need to speak with anybody now. Nobody should know our location. No phone calls, no emails, no matter what. It's me and you against the world. Okay, love, I love you. I miss you, I trust you. And I will call you back later."

I stayed locked inside his apartment the rest of the day. I ordered Indian food for dinner, but I wasn't particularly hungry. Later that day, he left another voice note, telling me to change my social media accounts to private. "Remove your surname for now, for just a few days or a week or something so no one will get to you with the name. Just to keep everything safe."

"You're scaring me," I replied. "I made it private, babe. I'm safe, right?"

"Yes."

"I miss you so much. How are you?"

"I'm okay, love, I'm with Piotr and the team." He sent me a photo of himself with Piotr, a somber look on his face. I didn't see the party videos that Pernilla had until much later; he wasn't sending me those or posting any of that on social media.

I felt so special because he trusted me alone in his flat with all his stuff. I didn't go through a single thing. I wanted to prove that I was honest. This, I now realize, he could later use to his advantage (*I trusted you alone in my home, now you need to trust me*). In hindsight, I wish I had snooped. I could have figured out so much, if only I had looked around.

Two days later, Piotr and the security team cleared Simon to return to Amsterdam. Piotr came back with him this time.

"Thank you for everything you've been doing for the team," Piotr said. I was too tired, too stressed, too emotional to consider that if Piotr were truly a head of security, with all the intelligence that he had, he wouldn't allow his client to rely on his girlfriend's credit card for safety.

Simon and I spent my last night in Amsterdam together, before I had to return to London for work. Now that he was back, all my anxiousness evaporated. We had a wonderful time together.

Back home, I called Lloyds Bank in the UK every day to see if the transfer Simon had sent from Hong Kong had gone through to my account. Finally, a representative told me that they would never transfer an amount that high from an international account into a personal account, because of the risk of fraud. Their response was enough to finally plant a tiny seed of doubt in my mind. *Is Simon really being honest here? Is he actually going to send me this money?* I told Simon what the bank had said, and he responded that the money was back in his account. It had, indeed, bounced. He would have to find another way to get it to me. I wanted so badly to believe him.

Then, on April 8, in the middle of the night, Simon sent me a photo that replaced any doubt I might have had that Simon was honest about his situation. The photo showed Piotr's bleeding skull.

"Piotr hurt. Blood," Simon wrote. I panicked. When he was able to call me later that night, he said they'd been out on the town in Amsterdam when they were attacked out of nowhere. The scene was pure chaos. He sent video of them in an ambulance, with a nurse with a Danish accent tending to Piotr. Simon showed me scratches on his own face and blood on his shirt, which naturally made me scared and anxious.

"I love you so much. Please keep safe and call me whenever you like," I told him before he had to get off the phone.

"I will, baby. I told you we were not playing games. I told you everything will be dangerous."

"Yes, you did. Just please keep me updated. I love you. I want to be with you now. I want to take care of you. I feel so bad."

"We need to be strong." We hung up and I tried to sleep but couldn't. The threats he'd been receiving suddenly felt a lot more real. The photos and video validated that everything I'd been doing was necessary, vital. *How dare I question his honesty*, I thought. *He really is in trouble here! The money is not coming in because the transfer was just too large. I'll ask him to send a smaller one.*

I was so, so tired. The decisions I was making weren't clear. I was living in a bubble where I was willing to do anything to make the problem go away, so I could finally just be with the man I loved.

Two days later, I received another flower delivery in the mail, with a stuffed teddy bear and a note saying, "My love, at the most difficult hour of my life you were there for me, supporting me and you're very important for me. Thank you. You're the best thing that ever happened to me. And I will never forget it."

Pernilla

Even though we weren't in a romantic relationship, Simon "love bombed" me, too. If I had a bad date, he would cheer me up. "Don't settle for someone like that. You are a special person, and you deserve so much more." When I tried on dresses and ran my fashion choices by him, he complimented me and made me feel pretty. He seemed so caring; he was always available when I needed advice or support.

He would do nice things for me, like fly to Stockholm for a couple hours just to have coffee with me because I'd told him I was having a bad day (in reality, he had another victim in Sweden, so he was probably conducting other "business" as well).

I felt he was a great friend, and I wanted to return his favors. When he came to Stockholm in early October, I treated him to a birthday dinner. He was gracious. "I really appreciate your treating me. Everyone always expects me to pay for everything," he said. "You're a real friend. Most people are only with me when things are good, but when things are bad, they disappear. You've always been so good to me. If you ever need help with anything, I'm here for you." I really felt I was important to him, which made me feel good.

He didn't just say these things on occasion; he gave daily reminders. Sometimes it was over a simple text message, other times a ninety-minute call. "Your friendship means so much to me. I will never let anything bad happen to you."

More than seven months after Cecilie started getting defrauded, it was my turn. I didn't believe Simon so many times that it's hard for me to understand why I trusted him about having security issues and needing money. I think it's because the links to magazine articles that Simon sent me were, in fact, real. I was at the cinema with a friend when Simon's messages came through. The news was all over Israel and some international media outlets:

> The Times of Israel, November 5, 2018
> Gem mogul Leviev is "central suspect" in smuggling probe; son and brother nabbed
> The son and brother of Russian-Israeli diamond billionaire and philanthropist Lev Leviev have been arrested in connection with a smuggling operation that brought hundreds of millions of shekels' worth of diamonds into Israel hidden in suitcases.

Simon's brother and uncle had been arrested, along with four other suspects who held senior positions at an LLD Diamonds factory owned by Simon's father. It wasn't until a couple of weeks later, however, that I really took the situation seriously, when Simon sent me another article:

> The Times of Israel, November 20, 2018
> Woman probed in Leviev smuggling case jumps to her death from Diamond Exchange
> Suspect had recently faced investigators probing multi-million-shekel precious stone scam; police reject claims they are abusing the rights of those investigated.

A bookkeeper for LLD Diamonds had "fallen" from the ninth floor of a building in the greater Tel Aviv metropolitan area, after being questioned by Israeli police about her role in the alleged smuggling. Lev Leviev (Simon's "father") claimed investigators had subjected the employee to severe pressure and threats that caused her serious mental distress.

"I don't believe this was suicide. It was murder," Simon said. Some of the articles I was reading raised the same questions. That was when I really got scared. This wasn't a case of someone just gossiping, speculating, or overdramatizing; it was all over multiple news outlets that arrests had been made and an employee from Simon's company had died. Psychologically, words that are published carry more weight. *They must be true*, we think.

The irony is, the articles were true—it's just that they weren't in any way related to Simon. How convenient, in retrospect, that the real Leviev family was going through so much drama right when Simon needed an ace in the hole. Once again, he mixed truth with lies. And he didn't ask for money straightaway; he built up his case over several days before hitting me with his ask:

"Pernilla, I'm really embarrassed to ask you this and I know that this is a lot to ask, but could I borrow just twenty-five thousand euros? I promise I'll pay you back." He explained that because of the diamond smuggling case, the company's bank accounts were locked, and he couldn't access any of his money. "I just need some money to get to a business meeting in Germany and then fly to Thailand to open up the bank accounts, then I can pay you back."

"That's a lot of money for me, Simon. Can you ask anyone else?"

"No, all my other friends are there only for the good times. No one wants to help me now." He'd been building that storyline since the first time we met.

> *I have a lot of friends but not that many close friends that I can trust.*
> *Not all people are good people. Many of them are users.*
> *You are a good person, Pernilla. You are a real friend that I can trust.*

I'd had a lot of users around me before, too. I knew that feeling. I could relate. I felt bad for him.

"Okay, I can loan you some of the money that I've set aside to buy a flat."

"Thank you so much, I really appreciate it. You are a true friend. Thank you, thank you, thank you. I will pay you back as soon as the accounts are back open."

I know what I did probably sounds crazy. To readers, it may seem obvious that I was about to get scammed, that I didn't do my due diligence. But I thought I had checked all the facts that I possibly could. I had seen a passport with Simon's name on it; I had seen bank statements, even real news that happened to his family (it just wasn't his actual family). Could you really fake checking into that many hotels? Checking into that many flights? Could this many people have been involved for such a long time? Could he keep track of all these different stories, if they were lies?

It's not normal to go to such great lengths to weave a lie, just as it's not normal to question everything we are told. We can't live our lives going around asking for proof of everything. Who would want to date you? Who would want to be friends with you? Who would want to hire you?

With the knowledge that I had that Simon was honest, which I thought was extensive, we arranged for me to send a twenty-five-thousand-euro wire transfer to him through Joan, his employee whom I had met several times. I was very uncomfortable about it, but I felt I had no choice but to help keep him safe. He had made it clear he had no one else he could rely on. What meant more, money or my friend's life?

Unfortunately, this was only the start of my nightmare. A week or two went by before the next request. Simon was still working and traveling, trying to get the accounts unlocked. "Can you send another twenty-five thousand euros? I am so sorry, but I have to keep working until all of this gets sorted." I was hesitant to send any more money; I didn't have much money left in my savings, and I had bills coming in. He felt my resistance and played his best card.

"The money is not only for me to work, but for my security. I am really scared, Pernilla. I don't have any money for protection. Plus, my enemies keep track of the people closest in my life, which also involves you, so this money is to keep you safe, too."

Panic creeped in. *My life is in danger, too?* I wasn't thinking clearly. I was already so invested, too.

"All right, I'll send seven thousand euros, but that's all I have, Simon." I sent him another bank transfer through Joan. I thought that would be the end of it. But the requests kept coming . . . and coming . . . until I was finally forced to say no.

When Simon didn't get what he wanted, he was no longer the Simon that I knew.

GROOMING TACTICS

Con artists such as Simon used to be called "love rats." They were the people at parties working a room to find someone ready and wanting to fall in love with them. Imagine how long it might have taken to go bar to bar, meeting people who appeared primed to be taken advantage of. Today, dating apps make it possible to connect with thousands of people who we already know are primed—they're on a dating app because they're looking for love.

Fraudsters are most successful when targeting victims who are at emotional low points. Some even read local papers or peruse social media, looking for obituaries and funeral announcements, divorces and scandals, company layoffs and general declarations of loneliness in order to scope out their next victims. Once a mark is established (such as a match on a dating app), the con artist sets about exploiting their target's emotions, lowering their victim's defenses in preparation for making their persuasive pitch. With our emotions at play, our logical thought goes out the window. Studies have shown that people in the early stages of love show brain patterns consistent with people with obsessive-compulsive disorders—the subject of obsession is virtually all they can think about. Any other thoughts are completely ignored.

It can be hard to recognize a con artist, because theirs isn't a hard crime; they aren't committing outright theft or threatening violence if you don't comply with their demands (Simon did that later in the game . . . but we'll get to that). They use soft skills—trust, sympathy, emotional manipulation—to get us to do what they want. All the while, we think we are doing it because *we* want to. We are given the illusion of being in control of our decisions, which couldn't be further from the truth.

Simon used many tactics to establish empathy and rapport with us, covertly grooming us to become complicit in his crimes. Because he was a "busy businessman," always on the go, his character presented a bit of mystery and a sense of unattainability. Human nature is to want something more if it's scarce. Counterintuitively, we become more emotionally invested the less we see of somebody (especially someone we have started falling in love with).

Although we met Simon in person, the majority of our communication was through texting, voice notes, and phone calls. Yet it still felt like a regular, real relationship because we were in constant contact. We were consistently updated with where he was, what he was doing; we felt in tune with his daily life. This constant bombardment (which we welcomed at the time) made him take over our thoughts. He'd concocted a recipe for creating infatuation (at least, for Cecilie). From there, he followed emotional tactics aligned with domestic abuse. He was a master love bomber.

LOVE BOMBING

Flooding You with Messages and Attention	Excessive Flattery and Gestures
Fraudsters often overwhelm you with nonstop texts, calls, or video chats, claiming they've "never felt this way before." This creates a false sense of connection and dependency.	They shower you with compliments like "You're perfect for me" or "I've never met anyone like you," alongside promises of a life together or elaborate (but often fake) plans.
Declaring Love Too Quickly	Isolating You from Others
Within days or weeks, they claim to love you, suggesting you're their soulmate and discussing marriage or moving in—escalating emotional intimacy unnaturally fast.	They discourage you from talking to friends or family about your relationship, often saying, "No one else will understand our connection," to control your perspective.
Showing Jealousy or Possessiveness	Manipulating with Guilt
Fraudsters may accuse you of chatting with others or ask you to prove your loyalty by focusing solely on them, building an emotional hold over you.	They use phrases like "You're the only one who can help me" or "Without you, I'm lost," to emotionally pressure you into taking actions—often financial.

Over time, Simon used particular phrases to construct arguments that distracted from the substance of what he was actually saying. For example, rather than directly asking for money, his first request was for a "favor." Psychologist Maria Konnikova says that "a good con artist uses the structure of his pitch to manipulate the way we perceive or think about something . . . he has power to influence your reality, the way you understand and parse an argument or proposition." For the con artist, she continues, "It doesn't matter what you say, in what order, or how. All that matters is that you say a lot, quickly, and that it sounds convoluted and has many moving parts. We tend to make worse decisions when we have a lot on our minds. Con artists exploit this by making sure we have to keep track of multiple things at once—multiple acquaintances, moving pieces, histories."*

By then, the fraudster has already woven a story; the more they transport us into their story, the more likely we are to believe it (and skip questioning some of the confusing details). And if we do bother to question the fraudster about some of the confusing details, psychologist Dan Simons points out, "A lot of con artists know that you might challenge them at some point, so they'll prepare for that. They'll counter what an objective person might say by warning you in advance, 'Somebody might not believe this, but here's why it's real,' and give you the counter arguments right away." So, when the crisis does occur, we've already determined, "You said this would happen, so I trust you."

In our case, Simon dropped clues about how he was at risk because of vague "enemies" or "competitors" and his business being dangerous. He also did something very clever: he exposed us early on to his lifestyle and its inherent risks and gave us the opportunity to get out. Under the shroud of "honesty," "vulnerability," or "transparency," we were manipulated to become understanding, supportive, and protective of him—to expect challenges and want to stand beside him through them, because *if we just get through this together, soon everything will be all right, and our shared dreams will come true.*

Because he chooses kind and caring victims, we don't run away. We stay strong, beside him. And from a psychological standpoint, once we voice a commitment to somebody, it's much harder to change our mind or perception. Konnikova points out that emotional

---

* Konnikova, *The Confidence Game*, 164.

impressions precede—and supersede—rational understanding. And here's the kicker—emotional impressions are *irrevocable*. Once we decide we like and trust someone, we are hard-pressed to listen to anyone else telling us we are wrong to do so.

And once we do something once, we are more likely to do it again—one favor becomes two, becomes three. The further committed we become to "helping" this person, the harder it is to change the story we've had in our minds. The fraudster feeds on consistency: "You've helped me before, so why not now?" "Just one last favor, and then all of this will be over." Our good qualities—kindness, love, honesty, trust, generosity—are used to the point where we complicitly destroy our own lives. It feels like being on a Ferris wheel that is spinning out of control: Would you jump out, or stay on, hoping that it will eventually stop? You'd most likely just freeze and stick it out, hoping that the problem will work itself out. Unfortunately, it rarely does.

HOT TIPS

Look for these common signs that a person may be grooming you for a scam:

- Acts of *love bombing*—going to extremes to make you feel confident in the relationship, deeply wanted, and the most important person in their life

- Majority of communication is through texting, voice notes, and phone calls, as opposed to in person

- Dropping clues about being at risk—and under the shroud of "honesty," "vulnerability," or "transparency," giving you the opportunity to get out

- Sharing stories (usually early on) that make them seem vulnerable, causing you to feel protective of them

- Keeping you on an emotional roller coaster

- Using language involving *us* versus *them* (the collective *we*)
- Escalated timeline—too quickly moving from dating to talk of marriage and a future, and too-early requests for a "favor" or money
- Making you think that you "owe" them (guilt-tripping)
- Saying a lot quickly, so that what they say sounds convoluted and has many moving parts

CHAPTER 5

Plot Twist

~~Why did it take you so long to realize you were being scammed?~~
When did you realize he had abused you?

Simon did everything in his power to make us believe he was paying us back. Between photos of fake wire transfers, reassuring voice notes, and confirmation from banks, we wanted to believe him. And we did, for a long time. But eventually the veneer began to crack.

Still, even after small seeds of doubt had been planted in the validity of his transfers or written checks or his word, we kept providing him money. We continued believing that everything was going to work out. To admit we'd been deceived was too much weight to carry, the consequences too dire. It was easier to keep riding the wave until we'd been carried so far, we couldn't turn back. When the jig was finally up and we realized we'd been manipulated to act out of character, immense guilt and shame and distrust followed—enough to keep most victims quiet.

Our stories and the psychological patterns we exhibited are hardly anomalies. We've spoken to many victims of relationship fraud who made similar choices, felt similar emotions, and experienced similar trauma responses. The psychological profile of our perpetrators was often the same as well. Psychologists and criminologists have studied this phenomenon; what we didn't see then, we have become experts at spotting now.

Cecilie

Simon's transfer of $250,000 had bounced; the bank confirmed it was because the transfer amount was too high (Simon knew the transfer rules and that if I called my bank, they would say this to me).

"Can't you just transfer a smaller amount for now?" I asked Simon. "I just need $26,000 to pay off the American Express." AMEX was calling me about my debt, every single day. It was the only debt I had in the UK. The rest of the loans I'd taken out were from banks in Norway, since that is where I had credit history.

My main bank in Norway, DNB, had already flagged my account for possible identity theft. Every transaction that Simon tried to make on my credit card triggered a notification, giving me a choice to approve the purchase or not. Now, Simon was not only constantly asking for money, he was asking me to manually approve his purchases one by one. I had never heard of a fraudster who would do this—allow their victim to see and approve every purchase they had made. And he was honest about what he was spending the money on: hotels and other travel expenses that allowed him to continue to conduct business. I had only ever heard of scams where someone asks you to send $20,000 to Nigeria via Western Union or something, and then you never hear from them again. In hindsight, Simon's strategy was clever. It's crazy to think about it now, how I saw myself being scammed in real time with each purchase, each approval I had to make. It made me look like I knew what I was doing all along.

A week had passed since he'd sent me photos of the attack in Amsterdam. I was concerned for his safety but overwhelmed by the amount of money I owed, which was starting to feel more and more like my personal debt, rather than Simon's. I was in survival mode: working full time, trying to chat with Simon and figure out a solution to my growing financial problems.

But Simon wasn't as concerned as I was. "I've done my part," he said. "I made the transfer. It's not my fault that the systems are bouncing the money." He tried to sound like he had done everything in his power to get me the money, although I knew that wasn't true. I didn't let up, insisting he get me the money somehow.

"Okay, come to Amsterdam and I will write you a check," he finally suggested. We made plans for me to arrive on a Monday, the fifteenth of April. I could sense, deep down, that something was wrong, but my heart was refusing to believe it. I wanted so badly for my early version of him to be real.

"I love you," I wrote.

"I love you more, my angel. I can't wait to see you."

He was at the airport, waiting for me at arrivals with flowers in hand and a handwritten sign that said *Welcome, love*. I had told him that I'd always wanted someone to wait for me with a sign. He had paid attention. He hugged me and kissed me and gifted me a pair of AirPods. *See, Cecilie*, I told myself. *He really does love you. Everything is going to be okay.*

But that feeling wasn't sustained over the rest of my visit. We had dinner at his flat, and he nonchalantly gave me the check. "Here you go." I looked at the check. I'd never seen a check before; checks aren't commonly used in Europe. *Is this real?* I thought. My gut feeling, way down low, was that something seemed off. But by that point, I was so desperate for some morsel of hope that everything was going to get sorted that I pushed the feeling aside.

Dinner conversation was strained. Simon was anxious: distracted and disconnected. He told me it was because of the business deal that he'd been waiting to go through, and the continued security threats. But I felt it was something more. He wasn't as interested in me; he barely looked at me. I was losing him, I was sure of it.

I returned to London the next day, where my first order of business was to deposit the check. Before I went to the bank, I took a picture of it and researched checks online. It looked somewhat official; it had an LLD Diamonds stamp on it. But I noticed things about it that made me scared that the bank would say it wasn't genuine. Something about the number pattern and location seemed off.

"Where did you get this check from?" I asked Simon. "Is it directly from Chase? I think the bank might question if it's real."

Simon got angry. "Stop asking stupid questions. Everything is fine with the check. Just go to the bank, nobody will ask you anything about it." By then, I'd seen how his personality could quickly change to angry, defensive, and aggressive, but those emotions had not yet been pointed directly at me. His reaction hurt, but I was brainwashed by then to want to please him. "Sorry, I'll stop," I replied.

Then he shifted his tone. "I'm sorry, baby. I can't wait to see you this weekend. I want to kiss you and make love to you."

"Yes, hopefully we can get things sorted this weekend. I love you," I replied. That weekend, Simon was supposed to come to Norway. We had made plans for the visit while in Amsterdam, after I told him how important it was that he meet my family and friends. Our communication lately had been 99 percent business and money, 1 percent personal. I was aching to feel connected to him again, for personal touch and affection.

I tried to deposit the check to Lloyds Bank in the UK. I was told it could take up to six weeks before it hit my account. I didn't have six weeks! I panicked. Loan and credit card bills were coming in nonstop. I called Simon and said he had to figure out another way to get me money, now. He assured me it wouldn't actually take six weeks for the check to go through. "Don't worry, they only say that for worst-case scenarios, but it never happens," he said. Then he had the nerve to ask me to take out more loans. "You will have the money from the check this week or next, for sure, and it is for more than what you gave me, so you owe me anyway."

> Cecilie: "Babe, I can't do more. Seriously, I need money this week. I've done everything. I have over $200,000 in expensive loans. You have promised me for weeks that I would have the money. I've been very patient, and of course I get worried."

> Simon in voice note, he said, with a tone that was aggressive and accusatory: "I have done my end of the deal, I have paid you the money."

Cecilie: "I haven't seen it, baby. That's the thing. I can't pay down my loans on promises. I've been sick to my stomach for so many weeks now, checking my bank every day, because I hate being in this situation. So no, I can't take out more loans. I'm sorry. I have done my best and I can't do more."

> Simon: "You can do more, you just don't want to,"

Cecilie: "Stop it, You're being mean. I've been helping you for weeks. Now you think I don't want to help you anymore, because I can't take out more loans? I hope you understand my situation here as well."

"I'm sorry, babe. I am trying to apply for more loans now. I really don't want to lose you."

> Simon: "It's okay <3 Thank you."

Cecilie: "I really, really care about you baby. It pains me so much. And I feel awful. I love you."

> Simon: "I love you too, so much."

I was so tired I went to bed immediately, without brushing my teeth.

The next morning while at work, I told him I'd been approved for another $20,000 loan. I'd been rejected by others; maybe by then my credit score had been affected, or certain lenders were actually doing their due diligence and saw that I had accumulated a massive amount of recent debt.

"That's great, can you transfer all of that to the DNB Mastercard?"

I changed the subject, telling him that I'd learned the date of my graduation ceremony in London for my master's degree.

"Congratulations, I will come," he said. "My love, how much is available on the card? And can you transfer the $20,000?" He was relentless. But then he'd follow it up with something sweet and hopeful. "I really appreciate the support. I know it's not easy times. It's a very difficult time for both of us but everything will be all right, and things will be better. I can't wait to see you."

"Me too, babe. When do you think you can be in Oslo on Friday?" I asked.

"Let me come back first to Europe and I will see what time slot I get." He was traveling by private jet.

I was so excited for this; he could finally meet my mom and my friends, who had heard so much about him. Thinking that Simon would eventually arrive on Friday, I booked a room for that night at the Thief, a hotel in Oslo I had always wanted to stay at. Simon had told me that someone from his security team had tried to use my card there the week prior (in retrospect, I now believe it was Simon himself) and that the card had been denied by the hotel staff. I imagined a foreign man trying to check into a Norwegian hotel with a card from a Norwegian bank, with a very Norwegian female name on it. It shouldn't have surprised me that he would have been questioned, but the reality was, this was the first and only hotel that blocked my card from being used by someone that wasn't me. That says a lot about the checks and balances implanted by businesses (or lack thereof). Still, I didn't feel I had done anything wrong—that incident had just been a misunderstanding, right? I didn't think there was any harm in using the card there myself.

Simon ended up returning to Europe on Friday, but then he started talking about having to travel to Israel for a business meeting regarding the hotel he was trying to buy, before coming to Oslo.

"I'll be there by Saturday, though, I promise," he said.

I went forward with my trip anyway. I arrived in Oslo very late on Friday, April 20, and went to check in at the Thief.

"Hi, I have a room booked under Cecilie Fjellhøy."

The receptionist stepped away and the manager came over, along with a couple other male staff members. "Hi, Cecilie. Did you know there was someone trying to use your card here last week?" The manager looked at me inquisitively but kindly.

"Yes, someone on my boyfriend's security team tried to use it, with my permission."

"We did not allow him to check in," they explained. "It was the only card he had, and this was very strange to us. A legitimate businessman would have access to more than one credit card." The hotel staff allowed me to keep my reservation, however. I went to my room and crashed.

When I told Simon that I had been questioned by the hotel staff, he insisted, "Leave the hotel now! That is fucking insane, I've used that card over the entire world and never had a problem." He was so angry that the staff were, essentially, doing their job. I told him it was a good thing his team was being asked; they were just trying to protect my card from fraud. He was insistent that I should leave the hotel, but it was late at night, and I was so tired, I just wanted to sleep.

The next morning, I texted Simon. "Any updates for today?"

"No, I will let you know when I'm on my way to the airport." My heart sank. I started to feel like he was never going to come . . . that maybe he knew that all along. *Then why did he count down the days with me?* I wondered. *Why is he backtracking, when he'd acted like he missed me too and couldn't wait to see me?* So much didn't make sense. But the deal came before anything else.

The strangest thing is how safe I felt with him, even when I had so many questions and concerns. When everything went to shit and no money was coming in and I was at rock bottom, I still just wanted to see him. It was when I was away from him that I felt everything was crumbling; when I was with him, at least, I still felt like we were real.

I was so embarrassed that he wasn't going to make it to Oslo. I had planned a lunch and invited my friends, and now Simon wasn't going to be there. They were all asking me questions that I couldn't answer. Later that day, I called Simon and put him on speakerphone with my mom, whom he was also supposed to meet. He apologized that he couldn't come. My mom was very understanding. I, however, felt a growing pit in my stomach that moving in with him, marrying him, having children with him—all the things we'd discussed early on—weren't going to happen.

I felt betrayed, not only from a financial perspective but from a romantic perspective. I truly thought he was my boyfriend. I cared for him so much that it still hurts when I think about what he did to me relationship-wise. Through Pernilla, I later learned that while I was waiting for Simon to arrive in Oslo, he was flying three other women from Norway to Amsterdam, where they partied it up together.

Meanwhile, I was still waiting for the check Simon had given to me to clear. I felt horrible every single morning, checking my bank account, calling my bank. I was being eaten alive, knowing what was awaiting me if I didn't get this money in. Finally, while I was in Oslo, my bank in the UK gave me an answer: the check wasn't going to go through.

"Your account is too new to deposit a check that large," I was told.

"Is the check real, though?" I asked.

"Yes, the check is good," I was told (spoiler alert: it wasn't). Once again, I felt stupid for doubting Simon. *Okay, the check is good. Simon didn't lie to me.* The bank would know if this was fraud, right?

After weeks of feeling beaten and battered down, I took hold of this one small hint of something positive, grabbed it with both hands, and held on for dear life. The check was real.

I also had another hope to hold on to. Simon had told me that the hotel deal was supposed to finalize on May 1. Just a few days away. The transfers Simon had made hadn't gone through, the check wasn't going to clear, but his stress with work would soon be over. We could go back to being boyfriend and girlfriend. Why on earth I was still hoping for this, I question to this day.

Until then, Simon and I texted and talked every day. He asked for more money, while I asked for any money at all. My physical state continued to deteriorate. His expenses kept piling up, to the point where I asked him to stop using my card.

"I can't pay any of this debt down, Simon. I have nothing, baby. My account is empty. You have to help me with this," I told him. "I'm really worried. I am not sleeping, and my body is breaking out in a rash. I need to properly relax."

"You will soon, my love."

Three more loans I'd applied for in a state of angst had been approved.

April 24—Sbanken, $20,000
April 25—Thorn Finance, $4,500
April 26—Gjensidige, $20,000

These were out of desperation. I was in crisis mode; I just didn't want to believe that everything had been a lie. Now I want to grab hold of myself in the past and say *Wake up, Cecilie! Stop pretending!* So many fraud victims describe the same feeling, in retrospect. They know in their gut they've been had, but the reality is scarier than the lie. I've heard that phase best described as being in the "waiting room." It's like sitting at the doctor's office, awaiting a diagnosis that we know is likely to come, that we don't want to hear. In the waiting room, we are safe—we haven't yet been told the crushing news. But as soon as we go through that door, we won't be able to deny it any longer. The doctor will give us the test results, and we'll have to face them.

My entire body was in knots; phone calls and messages from Simon never let up. He continued to ask for more money, transfer after transfer to pay down the credit cards he was using. I was scared that my co-workers would notice all the loan applications open on my screen or hear me on the phone with my bank. But they never did. Despite all the stress, I somehow managed to fully perform at meetings and presentations and hide what was really happening.

The only person I confided in a bit toward the end was my brother. When I spoke to him about the trouble I was in, however, I didn't mention that I feared it was fraud. I just told him I'd taken out several loans to support my boyfriend. The reality of the situation, that I didn't yet understand the extent of—the months of lies, fake friends and co-workers I'd been introduced to, fake paperwork, all the immersive theater—would sound stranger than the "reality" I'd been living within. Who would go to such great lengths for a scam?

Even if my brother—or my mother—had known all that had come to pass, there was nothing that could be done about it. The damage was done.

The evening of April 30, I was sitting at home, shaking. *This will all be over in a few hours*, I kept telling myself. I hadn't heard from Simon yet. He must still be in the meeting. He promised he'd text as soon as it was over. Finally, I texted him.

"I'm almost scared to ask how it is going, babe. I'm in bed now. Ready to sleep. I miss you so much. Hope everything sorted itself out. I'm so nervous. I love you."

I woke up the next morning.

"Good morning," I texted.

An hour later, when I was at work, Simon replied. "Good morning. I lost the deal."

"What?! I'm sick to my stomach now. I'm so sorry."

"Don't be. That does not help me."

"I just feel terrible. All that work you put in . . ." (It's amazing to look back and see that I again seemed more concerned about his loss than mine.)

"It's life. Sometimes you win. Sometimes you lose."

"I'm just so sad for you and for us." Really, I was sad that it had become even harder to deny what I'd been feeling for weeks.

To add more salt to the wound, later that day, I received a notice from AMEX saying that if I didn't pay $26,000 by May 10 the debt would go to a debt collection and credit reference agency. This would mean I wouldn't be able to get another credit card for the next six years. I called Simon.

"I need money to pay down all these loans. I don't have my boyfriend here. I'm in deep debt. And I have no idea how to handle this." I was about to crack. But Simon didn't care.

"I lost 73 million. I will appreciate some care. You should be next to me, not the other way around." Classic gaslighting, I realize now.

Then he left me a four-minute voice note about how he'd gotten into a car accident that wasn't his fault, and he needed to fix a broken tooth, and basically the whole world was against him.

When I described the desperate situation I was in, he suggested I take out a loan from my mom. I was livid. *How dare he?* I thought. He knew my family didn't have the money.

When I suggested other efforts he could make to get me money to at least pay down the AMEX, he rambled off excuses and, in a voice note, called me an imbecile.

"That is a word I never thought I'd hear you say," I wrote. "I love that you want me to just come up with fresh money on the spot.

And when I ask you the same, you can't understand how I can even suggest that."

Just when I thought he couldn't stoop lower, he always did. He continued to ask for more money over the next few days. His communication was constant and became controlling—I couldn't be busy, because that was when he needed me to be there most. To try to make it stop, I continued to apply for loans, knowing that I would get rejected. I wanted so badly to fix things, not only for myself but for him—despite my growing suspicion that he was lying to me. His health and safety and how he was doing were more important than how I was feeling. It was a very skewed relationship from the start and only grew more skewed as time went on.

As expected, my latest loan applications were getting rejected, fueling Simon's rage. "I've done this for over a month now," I wrote him. "I haven't eaten dinner for two days because I'm so fucking upset because I know you'll blame this on me if I can't get the money. We've been through this so many times now. And I feel I'm just lovable if I get money and that feeling is horrible . . . it never stops. It's like a bad dream. I can't wake up from it."

Everything I expressed about the toll the whole situation was taking on me was ignored and redirected toward him and what could happen to him if he didn't get money.

"This can happen to me," he wrote, then sent the photo of Piotr in the ambulance that he had sent me in early April.

"Why are you showing that to me? It's mean to threaten me with that. You need more support in your life than just my money."

Our conversations would go on for hours; I don't know why I thought I could get him to see the bigger picture or to have empathy for me and my well-being. The sweet, charming man he'd been in the beginning was gone, replaced by an aggressive, insulting, controlling man who was only concerned about himself and his current needs.

It was time to accept reality.

As much as I didn't like the approach AMEX had taken when they contacted me about "the use of my card," they were the first ones I thought to reach out to when I couldn't deny any longer that

I was being defrauded (I didn't yet understand that what I was going through was also abuse). AMEX was also the bank hounding me every day about my debt—the first debt I'd acquired—that I needed to address.

While at work on Friday morning, May 4, 2018, I wrote an email to Patrick, the employee who had first contacted me.

"I think I have finally realized that something is not right here. I have trusted someone as my boyfriend, and now I'm utterly terrified here. Could we have a meeting?"

> I think I have finally realised that something is not right here.
> I have trusted someone as my boyfriend, and now I'm utterly terrified here.
> Could we have a meeting?
> Patrick

He replied soon afterward. "I know of him and please don't be afraid. I would love to have a chat with you." We had a quick phone call. I was crying my eyes out. He asked to talk to my manager at work because he wanted him to take care of me until he got there; he was scared I might harm myself.

Fortunately, it was a calm day at work, and my manager was able to sit with me for two hours while we waited for Patrick to arrive.

When he did, he held out his credentials. "I bet you don't trust people anymore, so you probably want to see this." What I didn't say was that Simon had "credentials," too. Everything can be faked.

We sat down at a table. Rather than take out a laptop, Patrick took out a notebook, with questions written out.

"Do you have a picture of who you believe has been defrauding you?" he asked.

"Yes, of course." I took out my phone and showed him one of the latest pictures that Simon had sent.

"Yes, that's him. That is who we've been investigating. He is a longtime fraudster. You're the latest in a string of women he's defrauded." I pulled the scarf I had around my neck up over my head. The results were in. My body physically responded before I could mentally take that news in. I was shaking, sick to my stomach. I thought I might throw up.

I am justifiably angry at AMEX for the role they played in letting the fraud continue, well after they knew about Simon and the fact that I was likely a victim. But to their defense, this gentleman saved my life that day. If he hadn't shown empathy, like some of the other bank representatives who went on to call me "cunning" and a "gold digger," I might have ended it all right there.

"I'm very sorry for what has happened to you," he said.

"Are you going to go after me?" I was terrified of the consequences I might face for having lent Simon my credit card.

"No, we're not after you. We're after Simon." He saw how distraught I was. "Look, this is his job. You're good at your job, right?"

"Yes," I said, trying to catch my breath between sobs.

"Well, Simon is good at his job. He's a professional fraudster, 24/7." *He's right*, I thought. *Simon is a professional.* He must have taken notes on all the women he was in contact with, because he never messed up once.

Patrick showed me the names of several women. "Do you recognize any of these?"

"No," I said. Pernilla Sjöholm was on the list, but I didn't know her yet. He told me that these were names that had shown up on my AMEX bills. Simon had used my card to buy flights for these women. *These are all probably victims, too*, I thought.

"Can I reach out to them?" I asked. *They might not know they are being defrauded . . . or going to be*, I thought. *I have to warn them.*

"No, please don't do that. When this goes to trial, we don't want him to be able to use in his defense that victims were speaking to each other." I didn't want anyone to go through what I was going through. But I was too distraught to fight, and trusted that they would reach out to the victims themselves.

"What are we going to do about Simon?" I asked. "We can catch him. I know where his apartment is in Amsterdam. I can lure him there."

"We will silence him for you in a week," he said, meaning they would arrest him. "If you want, you can keep him warm until then."

I don't know what their plan was. But I assumed things would happen fast. We'd get the police involved, I'd lure him to Amsterdam, and he'd be arrested within a week.

Patrick left, and I went about one of the hardest things I'd ever done. I pretended that I still loved and missed Simon. It was heartbreaking for me. "I love you," I texted him.

"I love you, too," he replied. That was so difficult to read. I wasn't even angry (that would come later). I was just sad. I had ruined my life for this man, who had been lying to me all along, and still was. He'd never loved me.

Pernilla

I refused to wire any more money to Simon after making two transfers, totaling $32,000. For me, it was one thing to lend him money that I had in my bank account, and another thing entirely to go into debt for him. Simon wouldn't accept no for an answer, however. His communication became constant and more intense.

What am I supposed to do in this situation? I was so exhausted and torn. The pressure felt so heavy. On one hand, I wanted to help my friend who was clearly under a lot of stress and concerned about his safety (and possibly mine). On the other hand, I didn't feel it was my sole responsibility to fix his situation . . . he wasn't my lover, or my blood. Mixed emotions, duress, and fatigue kept me in a state of uncertainty.

One night, he sent me a text in the middle of the night on a weekday, when he knew I had to work the next day, insisting that I send him more money. *This is too much*, I thought. *This is not normal. A friend wouldn't do this.* I had a gut feeling that something was wrong. I started to suspect that he was scamming me, but I didn't want to believe it. Because if that were true, my entire life as I knew it was ruined.

It was almost imperative that I continue believing he was telling the truth; I couldn't face the alternative. Every time I got the feeling that he could be scamming me, I'd talk to him on the phone and feel so much calmer afterward. He was highly skilled at getting me to believe that everything was going to be okay . . . that money was on the way . . . that a "fix" was just around the corner.

As he was pressuring me to send more money, I was pressuring him to repay what I'd loaned him. Then, just before Christmas, he sent me a bank receipt showing that he'd made a transfer to my bank account in the amount of $100,000—more than twice the amount I had sent to him!

But then one day passed and then another day and another day, and the transfer wasn't showing up in my account. *There has to be some kind of problem*, I thought. I asked him what he thought was taking so long, and he insisted it was coming—he'd called his bank and they'd confirmed that the money had left his account. It had to arrive in my account any day now. If not, the problem was with my bank.

Again, I wondered if he was scamming me, but I pushed the thought aside. *That can't be true, it just can't*. He'd been my friend for nearly a year! He couldn't possibly have been lying to me all that time, right?

I waited several more days, then finally went to my bank and showed them the receipt Simon had sent me.

"Everything here looks good," the teller said upon reviewing it. "It will probably just take another few days. It must have just gotten stuck in the system." I left the bank feeling ashamed for questioning if my friend was a fraud. That guilt—and the teller's false information (that bank receipt was clearly made by a professional forger)—led me to losing even more money. Certain that the money was on the way and Simon was good for his word, I agreed to his plea to help him buy a flight with my credit card, so his lawyer could go to their bank in Bangkok to release funds. I couldn't believe it when the charge came through—sixty-five hundred euros! He had booked a first-class seat.

That money better arrive in my account fast, I thought. My anxiety escalated. I waited . . . and waited . . . and waited. I logged into my account over and over again every day, all day. Nothing. The sick feeling in my stomach increased. I repeatedly called Simon and he would calm me down, assuring me that things would get sorted, it was just some kind of administrative failure. "I am going to send another transfer right now," he promised. "Don't worry, this one will go through." He sent me another transfer receipt.

Meanwhile, relentless requests to use my credit card to book flights continued. He could sit on the phone for hours, still playing the role of a friend but putting a ton of pressure on me. "I sent you more than what you gave me, and that's okay, I'm happy to do that for you, but you can do this one more thing for me since I don't have any money now because I sent it all to you," he would try to reason.

Again, I felt that my kindness was being taken advantage of. The stress and anxiety made me physically ill. By my birthday, January 7, 2019, I was in bed with a fever of 104 degrees. And yet Simon kept calling, asking to use my credit card for another flight.

"I will help you, Simon, but not right now. After I get some sleep, I will call you." I would say anything to get him to stop calling and let me sleep.

"Pernilla, I am sick too. But I have to push through because this is a matter of life or death. This isn't a joke. I don't have anyone else to turn to right now and I really need to book this flight. Can you just give me your card number, and I will book it?" The pressure and constant messaging and phone calls that I just wanted to stop finally caused me to cave.

"Okay, fine . . . here's my card number. You can book one more flight on it," I told him. *Now please, just let me sleep!* Had I been rested, had I not been sick, I would never have done that. The feeling in my gut that something was terribly wrong, I believe, would have won over.

While I slept, he booked six more flights at $900 each. I saw the pending transactions on my account after I woke up. *What the fuck is this?* I could barely breathe. I called Simon, enraged. "I told you that you could book just one flight!"

"I did, those are just preauthorization transactions, they will fall off. Your card will only be charged for one flight, I promise," he said.

I didn't believe him. "I can't help you anymore, Simon, that is it." I blocked my card but lied and told him that AMEX had blocked my account. "There's nothing I can do, Simon, my hands are tied. They won't unblock the card until I get money from you to pay down the balance."

Not long after that, I received a notification that he had tried to use my card again.

"Simon, did you try to use my credit card?" I asked him. He denied it. Now I was almost certain that I'd been scammed. I decided to test how far he would go. The next time he asked for money, I offered, "I don't have any more, Simon, but I could ask my family for money." I would never do that. And I would never ask a friend to do that for me.

"Okay, that would be great," he said. "Can you ask them today?"

Wow. *Why would he think I would ever do something like that?* I thought.

Still, I continued to check my bank account, day after day, hoping and praying to see one of the transfers that Simon had made go through. *Please, let my gut feeling be wrong.* It was futile.

On January 30, I was at a work fair in Stockholm when I received a message through Facebook that nearly made my heart stop.

"Hello! I am a journalist for the newspaper VG in Norway. We are working on a documentary about someone called Shimon Hayut, but who has pretended to be Simon Leviev, son of Israeli diamond billionaire Lev Leviev. We tell the story of a Norwegian woman who has been duped out of large sums of money by this man. We have information that you may also be someone who has been in contact with him. Could that be true?"

My worst fears were confirmed. I had lost my entire savings. I became dizzy and could barely stand. I wanted to scream. How could anyone do this to me, let alone someone whom I thought was my friend? I was in a state of shock and wasn't thinking clearly; my instant reaction was to call Simon.

"Some journalist contacted me and said someone is scamming women under your name. What is going on?"

"That is bullshit," he said, anger in his voice. "My enemies are behind that. They are trying to set me up." His response was even more hurtful than if he'd just admitted it. I understood that his excuses didn't make sense; he was putting on a show. However, I played along with what he was saying. I wanted him to get caught.

I've always been prepared while in a relationship that my boyfriend might cheat on me, but I'd never prepared for a friend cheating me. Friendships aren't supposed to end this way. After nearly ten months! I couldn't wrap my brain around why he had waited so long to defraud me. Until then, I thought fraudsters worked fast: scam a victim, then get out. And why would he have chosen me as a victim? He knew my father had worked at Europol, and that I came from a family of police officers. To me, that was so careless of him, but in retrospect, he was being cocky and narcissistic; he was so sure he could get away with it, perhaps because he knew how corrupt the system is. Still, he picked the wrong victim. I committed then and there to doing everything in my power to get him behind bars. I couldn't let him do this to anyone else.

First, I needed to verify that what the journalist had said was true. I left the work fair and called the head office of *VG* to see if this journalist, Erland, really worked there. He did. Erland called me back that afternoon and we agreed he would fly out to Stockholm to meet with me the next day and explain what had happened to the Norwegian woman and countless others. We decided it was best if I played naïve and pretended to be on Simon's side for now, so that I could help the police find him and arrest him.

I went to work the next morning, attended some meetings, then went directly to the police station. While talking to the police, I got a text message from Simon. He had booked me on a flight to Munich, Germany; he said he could give me a watch of his that was worth over $100,000 that I could pawn to pay back the loan I had given him. The transfer, of course, had never gone through, and my constant pestering was forcing him to do something to calm me down.

I held my phone up to the police officer. "He's in Munich," I said. "He wants me to meet him there tomorrow." I was proud: so certain that I had done my part by reporting him and locating him, and now the police would step in and finish this guy off.

They would need to get an international arrest warrant, the officer explained, which he started the process for obtaining. I was certain the warrant would come by the next day. I would fly to Munich, meet with Simon, and the police would show up. *The happy ending to what feels like a movie I've been living*, I thought. Easy.

I met with Erland from *VG* and told him my plans. He wanted to send a camera crew to Munich to capture the event for their media piece. Would I agree to that? he asked. I felt uncomfortable with the request. I told him no. I liked him as a person, but I was so upset with everyone at the magazine—they had known about me for months. Cecilie (whose name I hadn't been given yet) had contacted them in June . . . and they waited until January to notify me? And Cecilie herself never reached out to me when she saw my name on her bank statement? I felt so abandoned, like I wasn't worth anything to these people. *They just want a good media story*, I thought. *And this other victim must just want attention.*

Plus, *VG* only published in Norwegian. What good would that do? I thought. Simon needed to be exposed worldwide. I wanted his face everywhere. If more people recognized him, it would be more unlikely he could continue to commit fraud.

Erland insisted, however, that I reconsider. I told him that if I were to agree to their coming along and filming us, they would have to do the piece in English. Otherwise, I didn't need them. He called the head publisher in the middle of the night and got permission—for the first time in the history of the magazine—to publish the story not only in Norwegian but in English.

There was another benefit to their coming along—they would install a tracker on my phone so they could always stay aware of my location. There was a sense of safety in that. I had no idea what Simon was capable of.

That twenty-four hours was a whirlwind. I barely slept. I quickly packed and was on a plane to Germany. Simon and Avishay—whom I was meeting for the first time—picked me up at the airport and checked me into a hotel, which was a different one than they were staying at. When I first saw Avishay, I thought he looked so sleazy that had I met him face-to-face months ago, I am sure I would have had an alarm go off that something was wrong. But when you've already been brainwashed, it's very difficult to see what is right in front of you.

We went to dinner at the restaurant inside the Mandarin Oriental, a five-star hotel where I believe Simon and Avishay were staying. That was the most awkward dinner conversation of my life. I had to smile and pretend to enjoy my company—someone who had just destroyed my fucking life.

After our food arrived, Simon handed me the watch (which, of course, turned out to be fake) and I placed it in my purse. When he started complaining about how hard his job was, I said to him, "Well, maybe you should try something else." He looked at me, then changed the conversation. I regret not having a recorder on; the magazine had asked me to wear a microphone, but I was so paranoid that Simon was going to find it that I decided against it.

Finally, dinner ended, and we made our way outside. *When are the police going to get here?* I thought. So much had happened so fast, I didn't have time to sit down and analyze how things might go . . . or how slow the system could be. I'd placed so much trust in government and law enforcement my whole life, I kept expecting German cops to show up and get this guy behind bars. But it never happened.

What did happen is that Simon looked up and noticed a camera flash. Then, all hell broke loose. Simon and Avishay started speaking anxiously in Hebrew. "Get in the car!" he ordered. I was still trying to play the fake role of supportive friend; I couldn't act like I knew anything about the cameras or why they were there. I had to listen to Simon, because that was what I would have done had I really been his friend. But in my mind, I was thinking, *Are they planning to kill me right now? Are they going to leave my body in a ditch?*

I got in the car and told myself, *Pernilla, you have got to put on the biggest act you've ever put on in your life.* My very life depended on it. My mission became getting them to stop speaking in Hebrew, so

I could understand what they were going to do and try to twist the story around.

"What is going on, Simon? Are we in danger?" He told me that someone was taking pictures.

"Maybe it was just paparazzi," I said. "You look like a celebrity." I tried to build up his ego, because I knew how important appearance was to him. It didn't work.

"No, it's my enemies," he said.

"What do they want? Are they after me, too?" I didn't have to fake being scared. Fear was written all over me, only it wasn't his "enemies" I was scared of, it was him.

"No, no, it's me. They're after me," he said, driving erratically. He had to be driving close to three hundred kilometers an hour, weaving in and out of traffic. *If he doesn't kill me, his driving will*, I thought. A friend of mine was GPS tracking my phone, in addition to the *VG* crew, and she later told me how scared she'd been—he was driving so fast the GPS marker would freeze, at one point stopping while on a bridge.

"Let me out of the car, Simon! I want to get out!" Miraculously, he did pull over and let me out, then sped away. I was grateful for my life but mad at the *VG* crew. How could they be so careless? Their camera put me in grave danger. I notified them of my location, and they came and picked me up.

I couldn't sleep at all that night. I was paranoid that someone was going to come into my hotel room and kill me. I locked myself in the bathroom, because it placed an extra barrier beyond the hotel room's locked door. Somehow, I made it through the night and back home the next day.

I was not only anxious and scared, I felt betrayed. The whole reason I put myself in that type of danger was to get Simon arrested. But the police never showed up.

Meanwhile, I was still pretending to be Simon's friend. I texted and called him like normal, feigning fear for his safety. I was keeping tabs on where he was so I could update the police. Every day, I called the police station and asked if the international arrest warrant had come through yet. "No, Pernilla, not yet." *How much longer can I do this?* I thought. Talking to Simon was so traumatizing, it made me ill. I just wanted to block him and be done with him. At least he had stopped asking me for money; he knew by that point he wouldn't get any more from me.

I maintained the charade for a week before I finally cracked. I couldn't do it anymore. I was overwhelmed by all the directions I was being pulled. I had to work to rebuild my life after losing my savings. I had to do whatever I could to bring my perpetrator to justice. I had to stop anyone else from becoming a victim and feeling what I was feeling. I had to heal myself.

"Would you consider calling Simon and telling him that you know he's a fraudster?" the magazine asked. "You could fly to our offices in Norway when you make the call, and we will record it." Looking back, I don't know what I was thinking when I agreed to that, except that I wasn't thinking straight. Why would I put myself in even more danger? My mental state was so fragile, I just went along with what I was told to do, because I had put my trust in the staff at the magazine.

I flew to Norway and confronted Simon on the phone. He denied everything. But then things took a very dark turn. Later that night, when the cameras weren't there to record, he called me again, with a proposition. I could become an accomplice. I could help him scam others, as a means to get my money back. He actually had the audacity to make that offer. His scheme depended on it. Plus, it had worked before—he used Joan, and probably others, as money mules.

"Are you fucking kidding me?" I yelled. "I'm not a low piece of shit like you. I would never put others through what you just put me through!" When it was clear that he could no longer manipulate me, there was no more money to make off me, and there was no way to stop the media piece that I told him was going to come out . . . that was when he became psychopathic. That was when the death threats began.

I didn't want to show him that I was scared of him. I acted strong and cocky; I didn't let him know what I was feeling on the inside. That I was scared I was going to find a bomb under my car. That I had thought about killing myself before he could kill me.

Two days after I confronted him on the phone, I blocked him. As much as I wanted to give him a piece of my mind, I knew it was not healthy for me to respond in any way to his messages, and I had no desire to confront him in person. Not only did I fear for my safety, I understood that there is no way to reason with a psychopath, sociopath, or narcissist; I would never get the answers that I wanted, and he would never change.

Instead, I focused on contacting the police and pressuring them to start processing the case.

PSYCHOLOGY OF A FRAUDSTER

There are psychological terms that can be used to describe Simon's character—*narcissistic, psychopathic, sociopathic, Machiavellian*, to name a few. These are all terms we had heard before meeting Simon but had never truly experienced in someone we'd met. Which is no surprise; narcissistic personality disorder, for example, is only estimated to occur in up to 5 percent of the U.S. population (50 percent to 75 percent more common in males than females).* The percentage of psychopaths and sociopaths among us falls within a similar range.

Simon displayed all nine criteria that the *Diagnostic and Statistical Manual of Mental Disorders* uses to diagnose narcissism:

- a grandiose sense of self-importance

- a preoccupation with fantasies of success, power, beauty, or perfect love

- a belief that they are "special" and can only be understood by other special people

---

* Jenette Restivo, "Narcissistic Personality Disorder: Symptoms, Diagnosis, and Treatments," Harvard Health Publishing, January 8, 2024, https://www.health.harvard.edu/mind-and-mood/narcissistic-personality-disorder-symptoms-diagnosis-and-treatments.

- a need for excessive admiration
- a sense of entitlement, which may include an unreasonable expectation to be treated favorably or for others to comply with their demands and expectations
- behavior that is exploitative and takes advantage of others to achieve their own ends
- a lack of empathy or an unwillingness to identify with the needs of others
- a tendency to be envious of others or a belief that others are envious of them
- arrogance, haughty behaviors, and attitudes

How does a person become this way? Experts believe that a combination of family history of narcissism as well as certain early life experiences can lead to the condition. These experiences could include being rejected as a child, excessive praise or excessive judgment by parents or caregivers, trauma, or abuse.

Psychologist Maria Konnikova states that narcissists are manipulative and will do everything necessary to preserve their image. She describes narcissism as one of the "dark triad" of traits, along with psychopathy and Machiavellianism, that are interrelated.

Psychopathy involves a "calculated, inbred nonchalance . . . or the basic absence of empathetic feelings." Psychopaths are unable to process emotions like other people. Konnikova writes, "To a true psychopath, your suffering means nothing. No empathy, no remorse, no guilt." She continues, "A very small number of people may have evolved to take advantage of the general good of others, fueled by the nonchalance that makes many a con artist what he is. These people don't care; they remain perfectly indifferent to the pain they cause, as long as they end up on top."*

---

* Konnikova, *The Confidence Game*, 21–23.

Dr. Elisabeth Carter agrees. "This kind of crime is the lowest of the low. In many cases, fraudsters only operate online behind a screen. They can psychologically protect themselves by not seeing the victim as a person. But romance fraud is a personal, face-to-face crime, so the perpetrator sees the effect of what they're doing and carries on. The criminal has to have a narcissistic personality, some kind of alleviation of morals or absolute lack of empathy at the very minimum, to conduct this crime because no right-minded person would be able to do this to somebody without distress."

Online scammers, who never meet their victims face-to-face, may be so far removed from the reality of what they're doing—it's just their job, after all—that they don't recognize the human behind the computer losing their money. They may also be under the impression that fraud victims get their money back—from the bank, from insurance providers, and so on. Or they may figure that Westerners have so much money, they can afford to lose some of it. For scammers working under duress—be it financial or physical pressure they themselves are under—being dishonest may in fact be uncomfortable. They may feel that they just don't have a choice. Some fraudsters have been human trafficked and are victims themselves.

For psychopaths, however, "lying isn't uncomfortable or cognitively draining, or in any way an anomaly from their daily routine. It is what they do and has, over time, become who they are," writes Konnikova. We tend to expect liars to behave in certain ways, such as showing signs of discomfort, speaking or acting inconsistently, exhibiting facial flushing, fidgeting, stuttering, and avoiding eye contact.* That's what we would do! It's unnatural and uncomfortable for the average person to lie. But someone with one of these personality disorders would essentially do the opposite—they are so confident in their ability to be believed that they look and sound believable.

Overconfidence is also a characteristic of narcissism. Simon was so certain he could continue to successfully defraud people and gain access to new money that he paid no mind to the concept of setting

---

* Konnikova, *The Confidence Game*, 38–39.

money aside for a rainy day. Simon's confidence that he'd get away with his crimes is baffling in a way, because he'd been caught before. He was arrested in Finland in 2015 and sentenced to three years in prison for aggravated fraud, having done pretty much exactly the same thing to three women there while working as an "arms dealer."

The frustrating thing is, it's very hard to rehabilitate a con artist. Sometimes they spend their time in prison thinking *How can I do it better?* Simon got out of prison, changed his name and his story, and went right back to "work." Unless he's in jail for life, his crimes are likely to continue, in some way, shape or form. (After *The Tinder Swindler* blew up, he was the first one to make a quick buck on it by making merch, creating small videos for a fee for his "fans" on Cameo, and of course continuing to defraud people.) This sad reality contributes to why some victims don't come forward. Why would they expose themselves and go through the trauma of reliving what he did to them if it's not going to stop him?

Psychopaths are bred by similar family histories and experiences that make narcissists. Konnikova explains, "The first three years of life play a crucial role in determining your psychopathic future—something stressful can interrupt development . . . a single traumatic event or a baseline of stress at home in school could make the psychopathic traits you were genetically disposed to more likely to assert themselves."[*]

Machiavellianism could describe Simon as well: "the ability to deceive, ruthlessly and effectively, by employing aggressive, manipulative, exploiting, and devious moves in order to achieve personal and organizational objectives." Fear is a commonly used tactic. So long as he was getting everything he wanted, he was charm itself. But when we confronted or challenged him with questions, he became aggressive. We were scared to upset him. If we didn't do what he wanted, we feared losing what we had built—what, until then, had been a loving and fun relationship. If something in his life wasn't working out, he blamed us (for example, he said we didn't get him enough money).

---

[*] Konnikova, *The Confidence Game*, 28.

Then, when his aggression turned to threats, we feared for our safety. If we said anything to the police or exposed him in any way, our lives were at risk.

All of these were behaviors we hadn't encountered before. We'd never had relationships with con men. Our understanding of a con artist was that once they got what they wanted, they would disappear. Or, once we confronted him with the knowledge that we knew he was a con man, he would disappear. But Simon never did. Instead, he hung around . . . albeit, increasingly more aggressively, with threats designed to make us stay silent or otherwise join him in his schemes.

We recognized these insights into Simon's personality and tactics only in hindsight. We were in such emotionally heightened states, so immersed in his ever-changing theater performance, that we didn't have the time or ability to focus on the bigger picture. We tend to make worse decisions when we have a lot on our minds. Simon didn't stay in one place long enough—literally and figuratively—and didn't allow us to stay long enough in one place emotionally for us to figure it out . . . until it was too late.

WHY WE KEEP BELIEVING

We know what you're probably thinking. All the signs were there. Maybe not in the very beginning, but certainly sooner than we admitted. We "should" have seen what was right in front of us—Simon was a fraudster. We were "stupid" to have given him money, right? It's easy to make this judgment when you haven't been in this position yourself (plus, the spotlight should be on the fraudsters and the tactics they are using anyway, not on what we missed). Among those who have, a consistent pattern emerges—even after we feel something is deeply wrong, we dismiss it. *We don't want to believe we've been deceived.* We don't want to believe that the mess we're in is real.

This basic, human desire for a happier, simpler reality is at the center of the fraudster's success. Some victims never admit they've been deceived; it's easier to keep right on believing, to the bitter end.

To admit we were wrong carries heavy consequences; the psychological costs of cutting our losses are too high. And in our case, the financial burden was too overwhelming to face.

Selective perception makes us feel better. Konnikova writes, "We can revise our interpretation of the present reality: there actually isn't any inconsistency, we were just looking at it wrong. We achieve this through selectively looking for new, confirming information or selectively ignoring disconfirming information." Changing our perception or our memory is easier than changing our behavior. Human nature is to lean toward what we've already decided is true; if a conflicting piece of information comes to our attention, we revise our interpretation of it to fit our expectancy.*

Simon cleverly took his time to deceive us and did so incrementally. By the time we felt something was off, we were too far invested to turn back around or evaluate our situation objectively. This phenomenon is known as the *sunk cost fallacy*, "whereby a person is reluctant to abandon a strategy or course of action because they've invested heavily in it, even when it is clear that abandonment would be more beneficial."**

The longer we've invested in something, and the more we have lost, the less likely we are to change course. Psychologist Christopher Chabris adds, "Once someone has invested money, time, or emotional commitment, what they're willing to give tends to escalate, because they are desperate to get that investment back in the end or discover that any doubts they've had will turn out to be a misunderstanding. That's a trap that's hard to dig out of. It's like telling someone they're in a cult and having them say, 'oh, I'll get right out.' Nobody does that. So, you've got to invest in not falling in the first place."

Dr. Elisabeth Carter adds that fraudsters tend to speak of a final

---

* Konnikova, *The Confidence Game*, 237.
** Zane Fleming, "Money Management and the Sunk Cost Fallacy," LinkedIn, April 8, 2024, https://www.linkedin.com/pulse/money-management-sunk-cost-fallacy-zane-fleming-e9zke/.

hurdle. "There comes a point when the victim is so stressed out and doesn't want to do what is being asked of them anymore and is perhaps wobbling about whether to carry on or not. The fraudster will start saying things like 'We just have to get to (some) point, then everything will be fine. We can be together. The stress will be gone. If we stop now, everything that's happened before will be for nothing.' So the victim aims for that vanishing horizon, instead of looking back at what has already happened."

It's true. We were so insistent it would all work out that we stopped seeing red flags, even though they were right in front of us. We continued to act as though our prior choices (such as taking out loans and sending Simon money) were sensible, and to reinforce that reasoning, we made the same choice again, and again.

Interestingly, financial ruin is not most victims' greatest of worries in the end. The deepest scars are emotional and reputational. How will others see us when they find out what happened to us? Will we be believed? How will their perception affect our futures? The relationship fraudster relies on our reputational motivation to be strong enough to keep us quiet.* Human nature is to care what others think about us, even if we don't want to admit that we do. Why would we press charges, when usually all we want is for the horror we just went through to quietly go away?

For better or for worse, we are exceptions to the norm. We decided not to hide. In that respect, Simon chose the wrong victims; after the initial trauma wore off, we became bound and determined to fight.

HOT TIPS

Here are some traits to look out for in a potential scammer:

- A lack of empathy or an unwillingness to identify with the needs of others

---

* Konnikova, *The Confidence Game*, 285.

- Overconfidence in themselves

- When getting everything they want, they are charm itself. But when confronted or challenged with questions, they become aggressive

- If something in their life isn't working out, they blame you

And another hot tip . . . if you have been defrauded or abused, the best decision you can make is to immediately cut off all contact with your violator. Don't allow yourself to be available to them, because you have been brainwashed and might get looped back in again. Don't attempt to confront them; reach out to family and friends and a therapist and begin the process of healing.

PART II
FIGHTING BACK

~~When will you quit fighting?~~
What does justice look like for you now?

CHAPTER 6

Law Enforcement

~~Why didn't you catch him?~~
Why didn't the police do anything?

Simon had already been in jail for fraud, yet still went on to scam us and others out of millions more. How is this possible? It blows our minds, too. Equally mind-blowing is the fact that we couldn't, and still can't, get the police to do much of anything, despite having so much evidence against him.

The institutions we believe are there to protect us are often not. Most victims of relationship fraud find that they're not taken seriously and that their perpetrator is rarely booked for their crimes. Professional con artists, such as Simon, orchestrate every step of their scheme so that their hands are clean, and the victims' hands are the ones that seem dirty.

Cecilie

When I met with Patrick from AMEX in London on Friday, May 4, 2018, and it was confirmed that Simon was a fraudster, I was told their team of "special security agents" was working on "conjoining cases," so it was best to let them deal with the UK police, rather than report the fraud myself. I felt uneasy not going immediately to the police, but I trusted their advice. (I know now that their advice was wrong—plus, what are "special security agents" anyway, and why were they acting like police when they are not? I still have so many questions.)

"You can go to the police in Norway, though. That's where most of your debts are anyway," they suggested.

The following Monday, I flew to Norway, seeking the comfort and support of my family while knowing that something needed to be done to stop Simon. I lied to Simon, telling him that my grandmother had fallen and I needed to visit her. I went to my mother's home and tried to maintain the façade of being in love with a man who now felt like my rapist. As crazy as it may sound, I felt cheated on and sexually abused. I didn't consent to a sexual relationship with a fake person.

I had to report him to the Norwegian police. I didn't even know the proper process. Do you need an appointment to meet with the police? Or do you just show up at the police station? This was all so foreign to me. My mom took over; she called the police station in advance and was told we should come to the station early that Wednesday morning.

I was greeted kindly, but once we sat down with the female police officer, everything felt rushed and unempathetic. I was so fragile; I was breaking down as I tried to tell my story, which was only addressed with broad strokes. No follow-up questions were asked, no details examined. She was typing as I spoke; as I sobbed in my mom's lap, she didn't even stop to look at me. It felt like she wasn't really listening; she didn't react at all or ask if I needed anything. She seemed to look at me as someone stupid . . . I had made a mistake, a mistake she would never have made.

I didn't know how important my statement to the police that day would be—that this was my one chance to get the case taken seriously. That what I said would determine the way they would process the case—or, if they decided to investigate what I was saying at all. What that officer saw that day, unfortunately, was just a distressed and disgruntled ex-girlfriend, crying in her mother's lap.

In the end, after our ninety-minute meeting, the report was one and a half pages long. How could what I experienced possibly be summarized in one and a half pages? The problem with filing a report while the victim is still in a state of shock and trauma is that at that point, the victim doesn't yet understand what they've been through. I sure didn't. I didn't call it an abusive relationship. I hadn't had time to read through the several months' worth of messages to see the pressure and insanity of what I'd been through. I also didn't know the terminology needed to make the Norwegian police care, since this was a cross-border case.

I had so much evidence against Simon—about potential crimes he'd committed in Norway! Why didn't they ask for his flight information when he came to Oslo, for example? Why didn't they check with the hotel, the Thief, that had denied him the use of my card? They had no interest in checking anything. What I had just shared—the devastation I was experiencing—seemed to mean nothing. *You lost your money, tough luck* was what they seemed to be saying.

I don't want to blame the officer. It's very difficult working in law enforcement today. There was very little information out there at the time on relationship or romance fraud. She hadn't been trained to see beyond the "facts." If I had come in as a victim of rape or violence, I suspect I would have been treated differently, that there would have been some level of compassion and empathy. Instead, my case was viewed purely as financial fraud (albeit by my "boyfriend").

Before I left the police station, I asked what I should do about Simon. "I really want him to get caught," I said. "Should I pretend that I don't know he's a fraudster?"

"It's best to just block him," she said. Her words came as a relief. I felt so weak by then that I was afraid I wouldn't be able to keep texting him.

When I got back to my mother's home, I blocked him. I cried while I did it, not only because of what he'd done to me but because blocking him meant admitting that the relationship was over. And not only was it over, but it was also never real. So much of my recent life had been spent communicating with Simon: all his supportive messages, promising me that everything would be fine, that the two of us would always have each other . . . well, he had me fully, but I never did have him. I had invested so much into our relationship, not just financially but emotionally. I had loved him, truly. The fact that the person whom I'd loved never really existed broke my heart.

After I blocked him, it unleashed the most frightening part of Simon's character I'd ever seen. First, I received a message from Piotr. "Why did you block Simon on WhatsApp? What has happened, he worries about you." I didn't respond.

> Good night Cecilie. It's Piotr. Why did you block Simon on Whatsapp? What happened, he worries about you.

Then I received a voicemail from Simon, on my mother's home phone line:

"You blocked me, I don't know what is the reason. I am trying to reach you, but you don't want to talk anyway . . . I want to tell you something. Take my advice. For every action from your side it will be a reaction. So why don't you contact me normally. Not just disappear and thinking everything is all right. So . . . just watch out."

It was him, but it didn't sound like him. It was so dark. I didn't know him anymore; he was a complete stranger to me now. I was shaking when I heard it. I feared for my life and the lives of my family members. I stopped answering the phone if I didn't know who was calling. Simon had my address, my mom's address. He had everything.

Immediately, I called the police. It seemed they weren't willing or able to do much about my having been defrauded, but now I had proper threats on my life. But when I reported the threats, the police officer who took my call again reacted nonchalantly. My mom even got on the phone and said that she was scared for her life, too. Why weren't they taking this more seriously? It couldn't be every day that my little hometown received a report of a threat upon a Norwegian citizen by an Israeli con man.

"We will add this onto your case" was all he said. I never heard anything more about it; there was no paper trail that I could see to confirm that the threats we'd received had been added to my initial report. I sent emails asking for updates and received no response.

Since I didn't trust that anything was being done about my case, I also called the Economic Crime Unit in Norway (ØkoKrim, which is responsible for investigating economic crime cases), as recommended by the Norwegian embassy in London. I had contacted the embassy the day I learned about Simon being a fraudster. I wrote them a message through their Facebook page:

"Hi, I think I have been defrauded economically. I got a message from my bank to contact you for a meeting on how you can assist me. Do you have time today or can I come early next week?"

What I received in reply felt like a cold shoulder. Their response was basically "We can't help you. Just get in touch with the police." There was no trace of empathy or concern for a human being in crisis. Their job, as I understood it, is to give Norwegians advice and help when faced with a crisis abroad. But as with the police and Norway's Economic Crime Unit, there was no emotion in their response. I felt like I was talking to zombies. I wanted to shake them all awake: *Please, do something!* I was treated like what happened to me had been nothing. *It's just money. Suck it up.*

My repeated calls to the police were just an annoyance. "Well, it's not me who makes the decision, it's the lawyer." They all seemed to want to wash their hands of the case, since it was a cross-border case and most of the crime wasn't conducted within Norway (although that was where nearly all my loans had been taken out).

This whole time, I was also fielding a barrage of calls and emails from banks and debt collectors, aggressively going after me for not paying my loans. If the police had taken on my case, that would have given me some protection from the banks, even temporarily. I could have at least had a bit of breathing space before it felt like they went in and tried to slaughter me. Simon's threats, together with the relentless, immediate pressure from debt collectors, pushed me over the edge, landing me in acute psychiatric care from May 11 to May 16.

After I recovered enough energy to start piecing my life back together, I returned to London and to work with a façade of normalcy but an underlying sadness. I logged back into my work email, prepared to start my day. I didn't have to scroll far before an email from Simon popped into view. It had been sent a week earlier.

> Warning
>
> To every action it will be a reaction.
>
> You trying to hurt me, you will get hurt, We know you . Your family ,your friends, Take my advice and back off,
>
> You are the one that disconnected, Don't think you Sherlock Holmes or something, You can play with fire but you will get burn , I'm not threatening you I'm warning you,
>
> Maybe you don't want to be my friend but you don't want to be my enemy, And you will get nothing out of it nothing ...
>
> U disappeared, I'm always available on my phone,
>
> No one disappear from you .
>
> Remember to every action it will be way bigger reaction,
>
> So you can imagine what will happen next,
>
> Good luck
>
> Simon

Another threat. I started bawling my eyes out. My colleagues came in. "Cecilie, are you okay?"

"I need to go to the police," I managed to say. AMEX had told me not to, but I didn't care anymore. *I live here*, I thought. *This is where the crime happened to me. I have to report it.* I called Patrick from AMEX to let him know what I was going to do.

"I received a proper threat," I explained. "I do not feel safe. I have to go to the police here." He agreed.

I was shaking as I entered the station.

"I need to report a crime," I said to the officer in the front room.

"You're going to have to wait," the officer said. I was the only one in the waiting room, with a glass window between me and the officer at the desk. I felt so alone. Finally, a female officer came to see me.

At the start, she was very unfriendly, just like the officer had been in Norway. But at some point, something clicked with her. I think she started to see my case for what it was—abuse. There was empathy and compassion there, which I had been craving, plus the feeling that what I was saying was being taken seriously. She asked a lot of questions, gathering details about the flight we had taken from Farnborough Airport. I showed her the fake check I'd received from Simon.

I was there for four or five hours. I felt like a proper report had been filed. *Finally*, I thought. *Someone is looking at this as a serious case.* When I went to leave, she gave me a card with resources for victims of domestic abuse.

The next day, I was contacted by a UK charity called Victim Support, which helps victims of crime and traumatic incidents. I retold my story and was asked if I felt safe and if I wanted security. They could place screens on my windows for privacy or install an alarm, for example. They offered low-cost mental health therapy, too, and immediate access to the Listening Place, a team of volunteers who offer free, confidential, and ongoing listening for people who are having thoughts of suicide. All of that, simply because someone—that one police officer—saw my experience for what it was. A night-and-day difference from my experience in Norway.

It wasn't until August that I got a letter in the mail from Norway. The Norwegian police had dropped my case. They first said it was because of capacity issues but later said to the press that it was because it had happened in London, so there was nothing they could do about it. Then what is Interpol for? I fumed. The International Criminal Police Organization connects police forces across borders to share information and work together to prevent and fight international crime. Despite Simon's having used my card in Norway, the country saw the case as international.

This is how criminals like Simon win. And how victims lose. I feel that the banks later used the fact that the Norway police dropped the case as evidence that my defense against them wasn't strong, or worthy, or even honest.

With the UK police, however, I received emails with updates. Two detectives were taking on my case. They told me they looked into the Farnborough flight I'd been on to Sofia, Bulgaria, and confirmed that Simon had used a fake passport. The updates became fewer and further between, however. But it was summer, I reasoned, and bound to be slower. I had an interview with the police scheduled for August 13, so I figured I'd learn more at that time.

But as that date approached, I was suddenly told the interview was no longer going to happen. Or that if it did, it would be scheduled for later. I was not given a reason why it was being delayed.

Throughout that fall, I was working with *VG* in Norway on the *Tinder Swindler* digital documentary piece. Thanks to their team of investigative journalists, I got some answers regarding Simon. Patrick from AMEX had already given me Simon's real name (Shimon Hayut) and told me to Google it, which is how I learned about his earlier crimes in Finland. But the journalists took things further; they sent me the court papers that revealed that Simon's daughter's mother—whom I had met—had been to court against him. I also learned that he had been wanted in Israel since 2011 for charges of theft, forgery, and fraud. The journalists even went to his hometown and spoke to his mother, who said she hadn't had contact with her son in years.

Meanwhile, I was working full time and periodically checking in with the UK police.

"Any updates?" Silence. I sent email after email. Every day that passed, I knew Simon was defrauding more victims. *What is going on?* I thought. When I called, I was simply told, "Fraud cases take time." But my gut was telling me that something was off.

In December, I was told that my case was sent to the Crown Prosecution Service (CPS), a public agency in the UK that provides legal advice to the police, to decide whether a suspect should face criminal charges. But at that time, I didn't understand what CPS was.

To this day, silence in any form makes me anxious. I'm certain it means something awful is going to happen.

February 2019 came, and *VG*'s piece came out and quickly went viral. *Maybe something will happen now*, I thought hopefully. I'd been constantly hounding the police for updates, to no avail. Even journalists were contacting the police. "We still don't know his real identity," the police said in their defense. I knew that was bullshit; the *VG* journalists had traveled to Israel and confirmed his identity as Shimon Hayut. I'd known that since October! *This is not difficult*, I thought, frustrated.

Finally, in April, over a year since Simon had defrauded me, I learned why I hadn't been receiving any updates. My phone rang. No caller ID. I didn't answer it. The call was followed up with an email from the UK police. "Hi. We're outside your house. Where are you?" I knew the police would not show up unannounced at my house for anything positive. Something was very wrong. The funny thing was, they were at my old address. They didn't have my current address, because they hadn't been in contact with me.

"Can I just come to the police station?" I replied to the email.

"No, we just want to have a chat, and it would be better if we talked at your house." I figured I couldn't avoid it. I gave them my new address. Two civilian-dressed officers showed up at my door on April 11, wearing body cameras. One male, one female. They had a warrant to confiscate my phone and laptop.

What is going on here? I thought. *Everything has been turned around. Is this the route they're going to go? Investigating me as a suspect?* A year after I reported the crime to the police? It made no sense. If I were truly a fraudster, I wouldn't have gone to the police! Plus, I would have thrown away my phone and all other evidence. If something had happened to my phone, the evidence proving my innocence would have been gone, too. I'd offered to hand it all over to the police one year ago but had been told they would ask for it later.

I'd been in contact with AMEX all along, and they never indicated that they believed I'd been a part of any wrongdoing. Yet it was the fake documents I'd sent to AMEX, regarding being an employee of LLD Diamonds, that had caused the police to consider me in on Simon's scheme. And I get that; I understand that they needed to do their due diligence and consider every angle, but they could have asked me for evidence before considering me a suspect. Why did they take evidence from AMEX without asking for mine? I could have given them my entire WhatsApp thread, with everything right there. It didn't have to come to this.

Instead, I had to sit through a ninety-minute good cop/bad cop scenario, which took further toll on my mental health. I sat there in tears, literally banging my head on the table. I didn't know what to do to make it all stop. This is one of the reasons victims don't come forward. There's what Simon did to me, but then there's all the trauma of the aftermath. To me, what came afterward was at times even worse than what I'd been through with Simon. These officers didn't know how to deal with a traumatized victim or understand how their actions could further traumatize someone. The entity that was supposed to protect me was the very thing that made me feel unprotected.

When the officers were finally done, they seemed to have turned off their body cameras and completely changed demeanor. "We know Simon is the true criminal, we just need to go down this path." Why even say that to me, after what they'd just put me through? It was too late, though; the damage had been done.

An interrogation interview was scheduled for May 11, 2019. Not for me as a victim or witness, but for me as a suspect. They had laid out the case against me, and I was now given the paperwork. The argument was that I had met up with Simon Leviev in January 2018 and we decided to defraud American Express together. That was their case, which they had built without access to the most important evidence: the communication between Simon and me.

I was shown the fake documents I'd sent of my new LLD Diamonds "salary." The irony is, I hadn't even read them before I sent them to AMEX. I'd fully trusted Simon that they were official documents from LLD Diamonds. That tells me I was not myself in that moment; I would never do something like that if not under extreme stress and pressure. I am shocked that American Express approved them. I am getting so much flak for it, but what about them as a professional entity? Why didn't they do their due diligence? The paperwork listed a New York address, but they knew my address was in the UK; it was the address they'd used to issue me the card. Why didn't they ask about that? Why was I just now getting asked questions, after already being investigated as a criminal? This all could have ended before it began!

At some point, I couldn't take it anymore. I stood up and walked outside the room, crying my eyes out. My attorney came out. "Do you want to stop the interview?"

"No," I answered. I didn't want to have to come back and go through this again.

"Then let's go back in there, and for every question they ask, just say 'No comment.'" So that's what I did. No comment. No comment. No comment.

After that, it was another long waiting game. Saying it was torture doesn't begin to describe how I felt. I had hoped it would go fast, that they'd read through my WhatsApp messages and quickly find the evidence that I had not schemed or scammed alongside Simon. Not so.

Then, in June, Simon was arrested for fraud in Greece for using a fake passport and extradited to Israel. At first, I celebrated that news, assuming the arrest had been conducted by Interpol, but I didn't know any of the details about it. When I tried to contact the police to find anything out, they wouldn't give me any information, because I was still a suspect. *I am not allowed to know anything about the guy who made death threats against me*, I thought, incredulously. They had taken away my rights as a victim.

The lead officer on the case would get annoyed when I'd call regarding Simon's arrest. Finally, he wrote in an email, "I can't tell you anything. See it in the media."

More silence followed. I was fucking scared. The thought of having to go to court or even jail for something I didn't do weighed heavily upon me. Still, every month I was contacting the police to try to get something moving forward on my case against Simon. Then, in September, I got a message from my previous landlord.

"Hi, Cecilie, there's a thick envelope here from the Ministry of Justice. I think you need to pick it up."

My heart started pounding. *Oh my God, they've indicted me*, I thought. I walked over there to collect it. I opened the envelope and saw all these Greek letters. Simon had filed a defamation claim against us, saying that we had "insulted his honor and respect" and made it difficult for him to have professional credibility or create a family life. WTF? If I hadn't been so overwhelmed, I would have laughed. Instead, it was one more thing to deal with, on top of everything else. Since June, I'd been going to trial against four banks (more on that in the next chapter). The pressure was insane.

It wasn't until about a year later, in August 2020, that I got a call from the officer handling my case.

"Sorry about the wait," he started. "We've closed the case that you had against Simon. But we've closed the case we had against you, as well."

What a juxtaposition of emotion: tremendous relief that I was no longer being pursued as a criminal. I hadn't realized until that moment just how heavy that weight had been on me; it was almost unbearable. I was trembling. I recorded that phone call and can hear in my voice how scared I was that I was going to be told I was being indicted. But I also felt vast disappointment that I wasn't able to pursue justice for what Simon had done to me and countless others.

The officer continued, "Don't be too disheartened about the fact that we closed your case. We do have another fraud case which Simon conducted against the transportation company, and we are going to focus our investigation on that. It's a far more serious fraud—almost half a million pounds or so—and he's going to get far more time for that than, unfortunately, what he did to you just because of the financial side of it." So defrauding a company was once again considered "a far more serious crime." What he said next, however, hurt the most.

"I had to look at whether it was worth prosecuting you in order to try and get to him. But because of your emotional state, I didn't want to put the emotional strain on you for it, especially if we can get him on another fraud anyway." How could he even think about prosecuting me in pursuit of Simon? What kind of emotional state did he think I would be in? What a horrible thing to say!

Essentially, I was the easier target. I knew I'd made mistakes and would have to face consequences. But to know that Simon had committed far more serious fraud against me and others and was being let off the hook was frustrating beyond measure.

That company fraud case is still going on at the time of this writing—six years later! And that is just one of the companies he's defrauded; think of all the private jets he's been on, and all the luxury cars and flats he's rented ("his" Amsterdam flat turned out to be an Airbnb; he scammed the owners of the flat as well, with fake checks and wire transfers). Imagine all the business owners and contractors left in his wake. But to hear that the police look at those crimes as more serious makes me so angry; there are no laws to protect individual victims of relationship fraud. Few fraudsters get sentenced for mental abuse; the financial aspect is the only one taken seriously. What they have done to us from the human perspective, he will never have to stand trial for.

Still, the overriding emotion I had after getting off that call from the Metropolitan Police officer was happiness. I was free from one heavier-than-shit thing I'd had hanging over me.

In 2023, I decided to file an official complaint with the UK police department for how my case had been handled. *They need to look back on this and learn from it*, I thought. The head of the Metropolitan Police sat down with me, apologized, and told me their process would not be handled the same way today. I felt seen and heard. He also answered some of my long-standing questions. He told me my case had been dropped because I had gone to the media with my story (the *VG* piece and, later, the Netflix *Tinder Swindler* documentary). Since so much became public information, it would be difficult to give Simon a fair trial in court. I had lost my opportunity for justice, in one sense. However, how many people are able to recognize Simon's face as a fraudster, and how many platforms did he subsequently get banned from, because I'd gone public? There are pros and cons to every decision. I still feel I made the right choice by going public.

I was also told that the cross-country collaboration was terrible, which made it a difficult case to process. On the upside, we've received information that there are currently active cases against Simon in several countries. He technically can't travel to any of these countries, or he will be arrested. He's holed up in Israel. Some justice, at least, was served after his ex-girlfriend, Israeli model Kate Konlin, reported him for domestic abuse and fraud* and won a lawsuit against him there in October 2024.**

In any case, my meeting with the Metropolitan Police gave me a sense of conclusion. I could somewhat close the door on what I'd been through, law-enforcement-wise. I've also been invited to hold several talks for the police on romance fraud and how to change the language, process, and behavior regarding how victims are treated. It's been amazing working with them. During one meeting, a police officer admitted, "Ten years ago, we never would have spoken to you because we thought we were the experts." The fact that they're willing to hear us out is a giant leap forward. The Metropolitan Police and the City of London police have since held several conferences on romance fraud and have shown me that they really care.

---

* Megha Mohan and Fay Nurse, "Tinder Swindler: Why I Stood By My Abusive Ex," BBC World Service, February 18, 2023, https://www.bbc.com/news/world-64666638.

** https://www.mako.co.il/men-men_news/Article-ba0cf044dc2e291027.htm

The *Tinder Swindler* documentary and the subsequent pressure placed on the UK police is one reason they've changed how these cases are handled. My hope is that other countries will follow their example.

Pernilla

When I decided to travel to Germany to meet Simon in January 2019, I was fully convinced that the international arrest warrant would arrive by the time I was in Munich and Simon would be arrested. When I'd gone to the police station in Sweden to file the report, I felt like my case was being taken seriously. However, that's not how it played out. I left Germany, scared for my life, with Simon roaming free.

Still, I returned to Sweden, certain it would just be a matter of days before the warrant arrived. I called the police every day. "We are working on it, but it's going to take time" is all I was told. Maybe . . . but to me, it felt like nothing was happening at all. When I came to the frustrating conclusion that it was not going to be a matter of days but instead months or even longer, I knew I could no longer maintain a front with Simon. He was calling me constantly; it was emotionally and physically draining. I had to end contact with him. I told him I knew he was a fraudster . . . and that was when the death threats started.

I applied for Protected Identity and was approved. In Sweden, data held in the Swedish Population Register is available to the general public. If you do an online search for someone's name, you can learn their address, phone number, what car they drive, where they work, what salary they earn, and the names of their children. But if you've been subjected to threats, you can apply to have your personal data restricted. This helped my sense of safety.

I basically went into hiding. It was the lowest point in my life. I started making fake posts on my Instagram page, misleading followers as to where in the world I was. I was so scared that Simon—or whoever else he was working with—would find me. I pretended to be in Stockholm when I was in fact hiding in Thailand. Wherever I stayed, I instructed the hotel staff to not give out my name or location to anyone. Even from Thailand, I continued to call the police and leave messages, asking for updates. One day, a female police officer returned my call.

"What's the rush?" she asked, no doubt annoyed by all my calls. "Walk me through what happened." I ran through my whole story again, grateful that someone was at least listening. But when I finished, she said, "Do you have any people close to you who you can talk to? Because it sounds like you have a big imagination." I couldn't believe a police officer would say something like that to a victim! I was alone in Thailand, scared for my life, just wanting to go home and feel protected, and the institution that was supposed to protect me thought I was making it all up!

It's easy to say in hindsight, "Simon didn't act on his threats, so you didn't need to worry that much." But what was going through my mind as it was happening was that I was helping to expose a large fraud operation, with a lot of money involved and a lot of people benefiting. If Simon could convince people to transfer hundreds of thousands of dollars to him, he could convince a criminal to kill me for a thousand euros.

I couldn't stay in hiding forever, waiting for someone to do something. I had lost all my savings and had already taken a two-week unpaid leave of absence from work; I needed to go back to Sweden and back to my commission-based sales job. To help remain focused on a goal and feel a sense of purpose, I went into full-on detective mode. When I first filed the police report, my case was written down, but I had not been asked for any evidence and there was no investigator assigned to my case. *Maybe if I send them the evidence, something will happen*, I thought.

After the *VG* piece came out in February 2019, Cecilie and I were finally allowed to contact each other. Once I'd heard her side of the story and understood why she hadn't reached out when she saw my name on her bank statement, I was no longer angry; instead I was relieved. We started a conversation on Facebook Messenger, which turned into phone calls, and then—just a few days later—a meeting in person, in London. When we finally embraced, we felt like we had known each other forever. Having her to talk to brought me a great deal of comfort, when no one else seemed to be listening. We compared notes, locations, and dates, putting the pieces of the puzzle together.

We were on a joint mission to stop Simon from scamming more victims. Cecilie and I started scouring Facebook, trying to find all the people Simon had introduced us to. To our disbelief, we found a private Facebook group for victims of Shimon Hayut. There were so many of them, going so far back! This was a way bigger scam than we'd realized, operating across many countries, over many years. *What did I get myself into?* I thought. Shimon Hayut had gotten out of jail in Finland in April 2017, only to change his name to Simon Leviev and go right back into business, defrauding victims all across Europe, despite being banned from the Schengen area under his former name. Even Avishay, his "business partner," was in the group, posting about how awful Shimon was! Either he was trolling Simon or he really had been defrauded and had gone on to become an accomplice to try to get his money back. Or he was just pretending to be a victim to collect information. Not even a support group for victims felt safe.

We weren't the only ones blown away. The *VG* piece spread like wildfire. Simon's image was everywhere. Many victims were coming forward, filing police reports of their own, in their respective countries. Many of those victims contacted us directly.

> I was also defrauded by Simon.

> I thought Simon had been my boyfriend, too.

> I saw your story with Simon, the same happened to me.

Through those victims, we learned the names of even more victims.

Meanwhile, we were contacted by several film and TV agents, interested in turning our story into a documentary. I was in such a fragile state, but Cecilie and I agreed to pursue that option, hoping that more media exposure would put pressure on law enforcement to take our cases seriously. It felt like we were no nearer to getting Simon arrested. It's not an exaggeration to say I harassed the Swedish police; I was constantly contacting them, submitting newfound evidence, asking for updates, trying to get a proper meeting with them.

I was also in contact with the German police. I shared victim contact information and case numbers with law enforcement from various countries, hoping that they'd see just how large this scheme was and corroborate information. But getting them to work together was so difficult.

I even traveled to the Netherlands to file a police report there, per the suggestion of a fraud specialist I had contacted in Sweden. Once the report was filed, I took a copy of it to the bank Simon and Joan had been using and got their accounts shut down. At least we managed to get that done, making it more difficult for him to access money. (In the *Tinder Swindler* documentary, Simon is shown broke, staying in hostels—a result of losing access to that bank account. This gave me some satisfaction and a little bit of revenge.) It again blows my mind that no other police department had bothered to do this already—that we had to do it ourselves!

I went from fighting mode to feeling like giving up, to feeling like I couldn't give up because others were continuing to get scammed. Finally, in May 2019—four months after I had filed the police report!—I was called in for questioning by the Swedish police and an investigation was started.

"Good work," they told me. "Normally, it's two or three years after a report is filed before someone gets an appointment to come in for questioning." *What? Why on earth does it take so long?* I thought. The months I'd waited had felt like years.

In June, my efforts at first appeared to pay off when I received notice from AMEX's security department that Simon had been arrested in

Greece and sent to Israel. I couldn't believe it. *Finally!* I thought. I called Cecilie and told her the news. We both started crying happy tears; it was such a relief that all the work we'd done was finally getting us somewhere. Justice was being served! We were in celebration mode . . . until we found out what he'd been arrested for: a fake passport.

What? What about the millions he'd defrauded people out of?

It wasn't long after his arrest that I learned that the Swedish police were dropping my case. "We can't get him now," they said. "He's in Israel. There's no extradition order between Europe and Israel."

The photos of Simon in handcuffs look great in the documentary. But we sincerely believe that Simon getting arrested for a fake passport was one of the worst things that could have happened in our quest to bring him to justice. We had spent months gathering evidence and submitting it to the police, waiting for the international arrest warrant to come through so that he could get convicted for all the cases he had against him in Europe and all the fraud he'd conducted there. It wasn't just my case that was dropped because of his arrest in Greece; I could only imagine how many cases in other European countries were dropped for the same reason. Why focus resources on a criminal who was unreachable? Perhaps if he were wanted for murder, things would have gone differently (but in my opinion, fraudsters may as well be considered murderers, because so many victims have died by suicide as a result of their crimes).

Instead, Simon was sentenced to fifteen months in prison for old fraud crimes he'd been wanted for in Israel. However, because of the COVID-19 pandemic, he only served five months before getting released. Five months, for all he did to us, and so many others. Five months, for all the lives destroyed. Five months, and he's back out there, roaming free and scamming more people. Where is the justice?

We haven't given up and are still working on it. Simon is currently facing a civil criminal case in Israel, brought about by the Leviev family for the misuse of their name, which means that if he does get convicted, he will go back to jail. Or at least, that's what we're hoping for. Cecilie and I are key witnesses in the case, since we have so much evidence against him—the LLD Diamonds name and logo on flight tickets, documents, fake bank transfers, and so on. Cecilie and I did talk with a lawyer regarding bringing our own criminal case against Simon in Israel as well, but the cost of going against him ourselves is too high, when we're already struggling to financially recover from what he did to us.

We get asked all the time, how come the police didn't do more? How come an international arrest warrant wasn't made? How come Simon isn't in jail? We had so much evidence. And it wasn't all only against Simon—he had accomplices, too, who are just as guilty of criminal offenses and are getting away with it. Simon wouldn't have been able to do everything he did alone. Why aren't they all in jail? We are the wrong people to ask, however. We'd like to ask the police those same questions. As you can see, we have tried.

To be fair, it's hard to understand the magnitude of this case. From what I have pieced together from victims, seven countries are involved, each with its own set of laws. If Sweden did come through with the international arrest warrant for Simon, within EU law, all the other European countries are then allowed to bring their cases against Simon to Sweden, so the criminal doesn't have to travel to seven different countries and attend seven different trials. That also means that Sweden would have to adopt seven different countries' laws, and what prosecutor wants to deal with that? Prosecutors are human beings, and human beings can be lazy when it's not their own money and well-being at stake.

My interpretation of what justice looks like to me has changed, however, since this all began. Justice doesn't always have to do with money. If Simon were to be convicted for his crimes and forced to pay us back, where would that money come from? No doubt from his other fraud victims. For me, that is dirty money. I don't want someone else to get hurt so I can benefit. I blame Simon and what went wrong in the system, but I can't put all the blame on everyone else; I also take responsibility for my own actions. Maybe it's to my own detriment, but I now see my financial problems as mine to fix.

Today, justice, to me, would be Simon being held accountable for his crimes by being sent to prison. It's not about what he did to me so much anymore as it is him experiencing the consequences of his actions and being prevented from defrauding anyone else. Justice looks like changing the way victims are treated, particularly by law enforcement; they should not be blamed and shamed or disregarded as "having a big imagination." Justice looks like educating institutions and the public about fraud detection and implementing company procedures for fraud prevention.

I do feel a lot has changed since the time when we were defrauded. Fraud is starting to be taken more seriously, because it is becoming more serious. However, I don't think most police officers are yet equipped to handle the magnitude of the crime, nor the magnitude of the trauma it inflicts on victims. I have heard many victims say that the crime wasn't the worst part of their experience—that it was how they were treated by law enforcement that pushed them over the edge and gave them suicidal thoughts.

CONVERSATION WITH AN FBI AGENT: MIGUEL CLARKE

To offer sobering insight into U.S. law enforcement, we interviewed Miguel Clarke, a former FBI agent and current cybersecurity expert. Clarke pointed out that a law enforcement officer's job is not to care for the victims; their job is to stop the threat, to the extent that they can. Therefore, when it comes to hiring law enforcement officers, desired attributes are not compassion and empathy; they are the ability to compartmentalize and go after the threat—to place handcuffs on a violent criminal and tolerate traumatic and gruesome scenes without having those experiences kill their souls.

"It's not that we don't experience empathy in certain situations," he said, "but they trained that out of us in work situations, because we don't have time to feel." Even so, the human toll of this line of work tends to catch up with every officer eventually, although it may take years.

"People tend to have very high expectations of law enforcement," Clarke stated, "but they're still people who, because of doing this work, have higher incidence of divorce and higher incidence of suicide. What protects them against those threats is being able to collect all the facts that they need for a case, while emotionally separating themselves from the victim." Officers are therefore not trained to provide victim support; victim support services are intended to be offered through a different entity. "Federal agents are limited by what the law allows for them to do," he said. In federal law enforcement, it is mandatory, for example, for officers to contact victim witness services on behalf of a victim. Victim support should, theoretically, then be provided accordingly. Resources, however, are limited.

In cases of fraud, Clarke explained that the officer's first job is to determine which statute of fraud applies. "If we can demonstrate that American Express was the victim from a financial standpoint, we've got a federal case," he said. What we learned from Clarke is that for fraud to be considered a federal crime, it has to be fraud against the United States, critical infrastructure, or an institution—it cannot be against an individual. Evidence from individuals can be used toward building a federal case, but the resources for pursuing individual cases just aren't there.

Taking on fraud cases is also limited by the fact that there are not very many fraud investigators, nor is there much training for this type of crime. "For financial crimes, the FBI Secret Service provides training for local police departments, but this is usually for task force officers who are aligned to some type of federal agency, who go on to get deputized as federal agents as well. It would be unlikely for a local law enforcement organization to take one of their officers away from working violent crimes and enroll them in expensive, specialized training, when they're already understaffed. Therefore, the likelihood of a fraud victim being able to walk into a police station and talk to an investigator who specializes in this type of work is extremely low, no matter where you go."

Furthermore, law enforcement officers are not trained to see things from a victim's perspective. All officers are paying attention to is collecting facts. They take down the information a victim gives them, then decide if there's enough evidence and enough resources to make it worth investigating. "If it's going to cost $40 million to go after $20 million of gold, no one will pursue the gold," Clarke said. In addition, "most law enforcement officers grade crimes on a scale of the worst things that we've seen; I'm not saying it's right, but financial crimes don't typically fall high on that scale." Both factors make it difficult for an officer to decide to pursue a relationship fraudster.

Even if an officer can get over all the obstacles mentioned and feels they have a case strong enough to make it worth pursuing and arresting an individual fraudster, they still have to get the support of the prosecutor. The difficulty in prosecuting relationship fraud cases is due to the lack of clear legal definitions and the need to prove intent. A young prosecutor will only take on cases they know they can win, Clarke explained. Elected officials, such as district attorneys, campaign on their success, so they need to demonstrate a high win rate. Only an older attorney, with nothing much to lose or perhaps an idealistic desire to pursue justice, would risk taking on a case that is as complex as relationship fraud. That's why this crime is so clever; there are so many hurdles to get past in the pursuit for justice.

Clarke added, "Given where our society is going right now in the U.S., I don't think there will ever be a law that will criminalize deception in a sexual relationship because that line is so hard to draw." He believes that the solution, instead, is in fraud prevention and education, and—once a crime has been reported—making sure there are enough resources available to support victims.

WHAT FAILED?

When we think about it now, it's pretty incredible that the three women in Finland who filed the case against Simon in 2015 managed to get him arrested and jailed for over two years. The number of relationship fraud cases that go to court is minuscule, because a lot of times they're looked upon as civil cases, rather than criminal.

The irony for us is that, because of this former conviction, Simon wasn't even supposed to be allowed into Europe at the time he scammed us. Yet he traveled in and out of the Schengen area for two years on fake passports and wasn't stopped! We had always assumed that if someone had been in jail in Europe and extradited to another country outside Europe, the possibility of their getting back into Europe was, like, none. But Simon was in the criminal underground; he knew the system and how to use it to his advantage. His time in jail was spent concocting an even bigger scam. He cooked up a new identity, got a few fake passports (relatively easily, it seems), and went right back to business. Proper security wasn't in place to stop him. The Schengen area is great for European citizens; we can travel freely throughout twenty-seven countries, without having to go through border controls. For criminals, this is amazing! Law-abiding citizens tend to believe there's more protection in place than there actually is (even at international airports). We feel less safe now that we know how the system actually works.

To our frustration, Simon uses the fact that he hasn't been arrested for these crimes as "proof" that he's innocent. "I'm not in jail, so I couldn't have done anything wrong," he says. Every time he's interviewed by the media, he uses the same argument: "If I'm guilty, why am I still out here after so many years?" And he makes a valid point; we are wondering the same thing. Unfortunately, the failures in our law enforcement systems send a message to the public that even a famous fraudster can get away scot-free.

Simon even, falsely, claims that he "won" a lawsuit against us. He posted the defamation lawsuit he filed against us on his social media, referring to it as "proof" that we lied about him. In reality, nothing ever came of that lawsuit; it must have been dropped, because we never heard anything more about it (Pernilla never received the court papers in the first place—they were sent to the wrong Pernilla!). You can't "win" a lawsuit simply by filing it.

Law enforcement, for its part, doesn't know enough about relationship fraud to be able to properly investigate these types of crimes—nor to properly support victims. How can you support a victim of a crime you don't understand? If officers haven't been educated to even know what relationship fraud is, they're simply going to place the crime in the "financial fraud" bucket and consider it money lost.

But relationship fraud is far different from phishing emails, clicking a text message, or ordering something on Facebook Marketplace and not receiving it. Yes, those crimes are annoying. You lose trust in a particular platform or the seller you bought from . . . but relationship fraud is next level. It's not merely a financial act, it's a human act. The perpetrators aren't just telling lies, they are the lie. The money doesn't just disappear from our account; a human makes us transfer the money . . . which means the evidence required for this type of crime is far different from the evidence required to investigate financial fraud. For example, our bank statements don't show fraudulent behavior—the loans and credit card transactions are all in our names and were approved by us (albeit through coercive control).

Investigators don't understand what evidence to ask for when it comes to emotional manipulation; they need to look at these crimes as they would an exploitative and abusive relationship. How would you get evidence that shows that a person's character is abusive or fraudulent (our WhatsApp chats, for example)? So often, we hear law enforcement say "These cases are difficult to solve" or "difficult to prove." The criminal, in fact, leans on that argument as well. But we believe it's a fallacy. Those are excuses for not wanting to investigate more complex crimes. The police could have done so much more, if they were using the laws put in place for prosecuting criminal acts in abusive relationships. Instead, so many victims of relationship fraud are turned away when they report their perpetrator to police. "You need to take him to civil court," they say; "there's nothing criminal that he did." But in Norway, for example, victims have no right to legal representation in civil cases, so they have to go to trial by themselves if they can't afford a lawyer—which, of course, a lot of fraud victims can't. That experience alone can emotionally break a person who is already feeling broken.

Furthermore, fraud criminals move fast; they jump from country to country or state to state, and each country and state has different laws. Collaboration between states and countries is poor. The transnational nature of Simon's crimes made it difficult to determine which country or jurisdiction should take the lead in prosecuting him (and the country that "should" may not have the resources to do so). Plus, investigators are hell-bent on doing things the old-fashioned way. Many fraud cases haven't been investigated properly because the police haven't been trained to understand how cryptocurrency works, for example, or data exchange technology. Privacy laws can make gathering evidence challenging but not impossible. Representatives from banks or other institutions sometimes hide behind Europe's General Data Protection Regulation (GDPR) privacy laws (which give individuals more control over their data and limits how organizations can use it) as an excuse to not provide information, when in fact that information could be anonymized and still carry weight. Compounding all of this is the fact that most laws are very old and not relevant to today's ever-changing technological landscape. All these (sometimes self-imposed) challenges slow down (or stop) investigations . . . and in the underworld of big crime that they're up against, you can't afford to be slow.

Especially after the *Tinder Swindler* documentary came out, we truly thought there would be more criticism of the police. As victims, we did everything we possibly could to get him arrested, and yet we are the ones facing the criticism. "Why didn't you do more?" we are asked. We essentially handed Simon to the police on a silver platter; we identified his real name, we could access his location, and we provided mountains of evidence against him. But "it's difficult to prove." *Have you even tried?* we wanted to scream. Yes, it's a complex case, but murder cases can be complicated, too. Drug cases can be complicated. If Interpol and Europol can collaborate on human trafficking and drugs, they can collaborate on this.

HOT TIPS

The language and process that victims use to file a police report matters. In the UK, for example, there is a national reporting center for fraud and cybercrime victims, called Action Fraud. The service is run by the City of London Police, alongside the National Fraud Intelligence Bureau (NFIB), who are responsible for assessing the reports and ensuring that fraud reports reach the right place. Action Fraud *does not investigate* the cases—that is the responsibility of the police, and the police don't investigate every report.

How a victim enters information into the online reporting system affects how, or if, the case is investigated. For example, one of the first questions you'll have to answer is what type of fraud you're reporting. If you choose "Investment Fraud" from the options, when it was actually a case of relationship fraud, your case might not reach the right people. Sometimes, choosing the wrong category can send your case into a black hole.

It's important to be very clear about the abuse element when it comes to relationship fraud. In addition to choosing the right keywords, a victim needs to know what to highlight in their story. If you say you felt "pressured" or "threatened," your report might be taken more seriously. But that requires awareness of the manipulation tactics your fraudster used, which may take some time to understand.

Here are some additional hot tips to help your case:

- Fraud victims can help the police by providing as much evidence as possible for their case. Law enforcement jobs are difficult; it is not plausible, in most cases, to expect police to fully dig for information. You have to do some of the digging for them, providing documentation that helps prove that what was done to you was, in fact, fraud. It's not criminal, for example, to not be able to pay someone back on time.

- If you go to the police with physical documents as evidence, they will take you more seriously than if you just come in and say, "I've been defrauded." This isn't fair, but it's where things are at right now. You also need to use police language to be taken seriously: for example, "theft by deception," and "I was manipulated and abused," rather than just "I gave him my money."

CHAPTER 7

Financial Institutions

Are you going to pay the money back?
Why don't banks have any education or protocols for fraud victims?

When Cecilie met with representatives from AMEX's fraud department, Simon's credit card of choice, they already knew who he was, what he'd done, and who his next victims were. That was a hard pill for both of us to swallow. The entire time they knew about him, they were letting Cecilie increase her credit limit (with false documents Simon created for Cecilie to send to AMEX, that AMEX never verified) and allowing our cards to be used to buy plane tickets in his name. They could have gotten involved and stopped this, but they didn't.

Because the loans and credit card transactions are in our names, the debt belongs to us, and every creditor remained set on getting their money from us, regardless of their own culpability and inaction. Trying to prove our stories to banks, creditors, and the justice system has been a nightmare. Those experiences turned out to be more traumatic than the fraud itself. But we learned a lot. Most pointedly: financial institutions may market themselves as having safe and fair practices that protect consumers from fraud . . . but sometimes it's all an illusion. It can be a dirty, dirty business.

Cecilie

When I met with AMEX and they said to me, "We're not after you, we're after Simon," I was so relieved. I was further relieved when they said I wouldn't have to worry about the $26,000 in debt I had on my credit card—at least not for now. I had bigger fires to put out: over $200,000 in debt that I owed to eight Norwegian creditors.

I was told by banks that the moment we realize we've been defrauded, the proper thing to do is to immediately call the bank and let them know. When I realized Simon was a fraudster, do you think calling the banks was the first thing on my mind? No, it wasn't. I had gotten in touch with my contact at AMEX in the UK, where I lived and already had a direct contact to reach out to, but I was not in the headspace to call eight banks in Norway. The idea alone was overwhelming, on top of all the emotional trauma I was experiencing in the wake of this giant shitstorm.

After I reported Simon to the police in Norway, five days after my meeting with AMEX, I went home and summoned the courage to go through all my emails and write down each of the loans I had taken out and the customer service numbers I needed to call. When I looked at the list, my entire body collapsed. I had to lie down. *What the fuck just happened?* I thought. I couldn't process it all. And I couldn't make a single phone call.

Thank God for my mom. She took that list and called every number, doing her best to explain what had happened, without fully understanding it herself. What most of the banks said was that she needed to send an email with a written statement of what had happened, along with a copy of the Norwegian police report I'd filed. I wrote a short email explanation: "I've been defrauded by someone I thought was my boyfriend." Then I asked for them to at least temporarily freeze the interest on the loans. I needed a little breathing space until I could figure out how to manage the mess I was in.

Some creditors gave me temporary relief, but not all of them. I was sent confirmation of receipt about the activity being fraud but continued to receive invoices and relentless calls, reminding me of payments due. If it were just one loan I'd taken out, perhaps I wouldn't have felt so desperate; it was all the loans together that was breaking me. Put the pressure from the banks and my experience with the police together, and that—even more than what Simon did to me—left me feeling like I had no choice but to end my life, which is how I ended up in the acute psychiatric ward in May 2018. I gave my mom power of attorney so she could speak on my behalf with the banks, because I was too weak. She was on the phone crying. "The woman you are hounding is in acute psychiatric care, and yet you keep calling and emailing. I won't have a daughter if you continue. Can you please lay off some of the pressure?" I can't imagine how desperate she must have felt.

After I returned home, I asked the bank if I could simply delay the down payment and received heartless replies.

> We are referring to our phone conversation and the email you sent where you asked to delay the down payment on the loan. Even though we understand you are in a difficult situation, we can't grant you this, since this loan was taken up just some weeks ago. We have to ask you to pay when the invoices are sent to you.

No empathy. No simple expression of concern. I felt they didn't care that I was having a mental health crisis and was suicidal. Sure, these are big banks, but there are humans behind the desks, on the other end of the call. What if it was their daughter or mom in this situation? How would they handle the situation then?

Without my mom, I'm not sure if I could have made it through that time. She continued to manage communication with the banks after I returned to London. When I came back to Norway a few weeks later, she looked at me and said, "Cecilie, they are not backing down. They are not willing to give you a break." There's no process that creditors have to follow in situations such as this; they could decide for themselves if I was a victim or a criminal. They all pretty much decided I wasn't a victim.

My mom explained that the flat I owned and was renting out in Norway was my biggest, if not only, asset, and the first thing the banks would go after. I knew she was right. If I was going to have any hope of securing money from my flat, I would have to sell it. That crushed me; I was so proud of my flat. I'd bought it four years before with money I had worked so hard to save. But I knew the situation I was in, and I would rather sell it and have the surplus for me to decide what to do with than have a bank foreclose on my flat and take the money, before a verdict in my police case had even been reached. The pressure they put me under didn't make sense to me; why were they moving so quickly to take everything I had?

A real estate agent who had sold another flat identical to mine just a couple of weeks earlier took on the listing. My tenant had to quickly move out, and my mom helped me get the flat ready for viewings. I had always thought that when the time came to sell my flat, it would be a joyous occasion. It was my first flat, and it had earned about $80,000 in equity. That is something I wanted to celebrate, but instead all I could focus on was getting it sold as fast as I could so I wouldn't lose that money entirely.

Within a few weeks, I accepted an offer. The money I earned from the sale went directly to my Norwegian bank account that had held my mortgage and one of my loans. I was so scared that I wouldn't be able to transfer that money, since they would see that I owed them $12,500. But I managed to quickly make the transfer using a cloud-operated service. The moment the transfer went through, I breathed a sigh of relief. At least I had managed to hold on to something.

People have all sorts of opinions about my choice to sell the flat. But that $80,000 would not even have been enough to pay the debts that I had. Fifty thousand dollars could have paid off one creditor, but I had seven left. I still would have been left with over $110,000 in debt, accruing interest at 20 percent. With the money from the sale, I could at least have something to negotiate with.

I wasn't strong enough to handle any of my finances that first year. The invoices continued to come in, but I put them on the back burner. My creditors were in Norway, and I was working and living in London, while also filming the documentary for *VG*, which I hoped would make the creditors realize what I'd been through. I still held hope that I'd be seen for what I was—a victim of fraud—and that my debts would be forgiven.

I had eight creditors and nine loans; with one bank, I had both a credit card and a loan. Each creditor asked for documentation, which my mom submitted, that a tribunal would review to determine if our case had merit. But every single time, the council threw our case out, saying it was too complicated for them to handle, and I just needed to pay the money.

There was so much I was expected to know but didn't. At the end of May 2018, when I called a low-cost legal helpline and mentioned that I had been pressured and threatened, I was told that there's an old law in Norway called Section 28 that states that "if a declaration of intent has been unlawfully forced by violence against a person or by threats that caused a justified fear of someone's life and health, it does not bind the person who made it," allowing me to contest the loans.

"That applies to me!" I said, relieved. I wrote back to each bank and said I wanted to use that law. When I'd first written the banks in early May, I had simply said I had been defrauded. I didn't know about this law or that it applied to me, and that I needed to state that. But one by one, the banks came back and said, "You are telling us this too late. You should have said it immediately."

They used the argument that the law also states if someone "wishes to invoke the compulsion," they must "notify him without undue delay, after the compulsion is over. Otherwise, he is bound by the declaration."

I wanted to scream at them, "How would I have known to do this? Do you know all the laws in the country?"

One bank, Gjensidige Bank, did come forward and forgive my $20,000 loan. The incredible representative whom I spoke with from that bank had previously worked with Europol and Interpol and understood the crime. "You were under pressure and received threats, and we have evidence of that," he said. He'd called Europol and confirmed that Simon was a longtime fraudster. "Forgiving the debt is the right thing to do," he said. He and his team in the bank had come to the logical conclusion that it made no sense to go after someone who didn't have any money; the bank would spend more money hiring lawyers to work on the case than the actual amount of debt that I owed.

By then, the *VG* documentary had come out, so our story was more public. A news article was published saying that one bank had forgiven my debt. The reporter had reached out to the remaining banks and asked if they were going to forgive the debt as well, and they all said no. Now my case became about setting an example.

There was silence for a while. I continued working full time and dealing with the pressure of the police investigation. It was mid-June 2019 when my mom called me. Somehow, I sensed she wasn't calling with good news. I stepped outside my office to take the call. "Honey, I'm so sorry to tell you this, but four banks have come together and filed a lawsuit against you. They are taking you to court." It was one of many times that year that my heart dropped to the floor. I started crying. It was such a heavy message to get; I never, ever thought things would come to that. Since the Norwegian police had dropped my case against Simon, the banks could go all in on me (if there's an active investigation, they have to stay off). At that point, what I had to do with the money I had earned from the sale of my flat became clear: it would go toward legal fees to defend myself.

Why did some banks decide to file the lawsuit, but others not? To me, it's obvious they all communicated with each other, weighing the pros and cons. Since DNB oversaw all my banking transactions and could see all the loans going in and out (over $200,000 quickly went in and out of my account), red flags that I was being defrauded were all over the place, and they did nothing. If they joined the lawsuit, they knew I'd be able to ask about their questionable fraud detection routines.

Among the others, if the idea of forgiving my debt was suggested, it was likely argued, "If we forgive Cecilie's debt, so many others will come forward and expect the same." My story was already public;

they didn't want that message out there. But although relationship fraud is becoming more and more common, it wasn't back then. My story was a wild anomaly. If relationship fraud was seen as a significant, growing issue, wouldn't that force positive change in banking practices to avoid further fraud in the future? They didn't want to view fraud as a wider societal issue . . . they only cared about their immediate bottom line.

In hindsight, I regret not being able to negotiate payment terms with each bank when I had the chance; some of the banks had also wanted to come to an agreement before going to trial (if we had come to an agreement, I wouldn't have been able to use the Section 28 law in my defense). I was hoping that the $80,000 from the sale of my flat might be enough to make a dent in the $250,000 that I owed, but it wasn't clear if it would be sufficient, especially with some banks moving quicker than others to send debts to collection. I was dealing with the police, feeling scared and lost, and didn't know that private debt negotiators could have helped. Perhaps a settlement could have been reached, sparing me the lengthy, costly court battles that followed. But instead of working toward a resolution, the banks pursued me relentlessly.

Each bank wanted the full amount due, no exceptions. "We maintain our claim because the borrower has provided BankID and a password themselves when creating a loan," they said. I hired two lawyers; I had no other choice. My legal team was fantastic. They were honest with me from the start about the difficulties that lay ahead. They were going to try to argue that that old law (Section 28) applied, with no examples of similar cases to work with. The only case example they had was of a man who was walking down the street when someone threatened him to withdraw money from an ATM—a crime that was very sudden and very short, with an obvious physical threat upon the victim. My case, of course, was more psychological and over a longer period of time.

To me, a crime conducted over a longer period is worse; it invokes more psychological damage and involves several more transactions (and therefore more money lost). But to the banks, a longer crime just meant I had more time to "wake up." That is the argument, at least, that they used in court. At the time, I had no way to explain the psychological pressure I'd been under; there was no academic research on relationship fraud. I didn't know terms like *coercive control*, or *gaslighting*, or *sunk cost fallacy*. I had medical records showing that I'd been in the acute psychiatric ward and had gone to therapy, but I didn't have anyone there to explain how it is mentally to be in that type of relationship. All they wanted to talk about in court was the financial piece.

I had never in my life been so nervous and stressed out as I was when walking into that courtroom in January 2020. I had rashes all over my face. It felt like an out-of-body experience, having to stand trial as if I were the central criminal in the story. None of that made sense to me . . . where was Simon, the real criminal, in all of this?

My mom came on as a witness, since she had dealt with the banks as my power of attorney. As she was being cross-examined, she said, "If it wasn't for me, you wouldn't have anyone to go after. Cecilie would be dead." They didn't seem to care. Pernilla testified on my behalf, saying that Simon had done the same thing to her . . . that this wasn't some crazy story I made up, it was a pattern he conducted as a professional fraudster. My best friend testified as well (although that backfired on me, as we'll see later).

The only evidence the plaintiffs had was my evidence—my WhatsApp chat, my witnesses. They filed a lawsuit against me without a single piece of their own evidence. For example, they used the fact that AMEX had contacted me earlier "about the use of my card" to show that I understood I was being defrauded and yet continued taking out loans. This narrative that fraud victims know we're being defrauded and just continue to give is wrong. Yes, I gave Simon my card, but I didn't know I was being defrauded. Something in my gut may have felt something was off toward the end, but by then the damage was already done.

The narrative in the courtroom was that I was a gold digger; a lawyer for the banks said outright that I wanted a rich boyfriend. My entire private life with someone I had loved was dissected and judged, and I was labeled gullible and greedy. They also called me "cunning," as if I were sitting in my bedroom, hunting for loans, looking for prey. In reality, searching for loans (especially high-interest loans) in Norway is very simple. You can do one search on one site and get numerous loan offers; you apply and then boom, two days later you have the money. But I was "cunning" because I had applied for a loan three times with the same bank (once directly, and twice more through mass loan application strategies—the latter two of which got denied). If I was cunning, why on earth would I try to apply multiple times with the same bank? Doesn't that show desperation instead? And how could I be a naïve gold digger who wanted a rich boyfriend, but also cunning—smart enough to sneakily get money from banks? These two traits don't correlate.

But my explanations didn't matter. Whatever I did or said, I was a bad person. They were trying to conduct character assassination. They had to prove that I could have chosen differently. When I argued that Simon had placed me under pressure due to his security threats, they fired back:

"Why didn't you ask him to go into a bunker for safety?" (because he was being pursued by "enemies")

"Why did you feel it was okay that he continued to travel?"

"Why was the use of your card so important to him?"

"Why did you believe him?"

It's easy to ask all those questions in hindsight, but I tried to explain where my headspace was at the time. They weren't interested in considering my side, however. Their attacks were relentless; they even barred me from emotional support by not allowing my mom to sit in the courtroom.

Their legal team even conducted an online search on my entire family, to try to dig up dirt. They found an article my mom was quoted in from eight or so years before, where she mentioned having been contacted by an online scammer; she recognized that it was a scam and did not send money, she said. They used that as "evidence," saying something about how being contacted by scammers "ran in the family," that this article was proof that I knew about fraud and should have seen what Simon was doing for what it was.

The trial lasted about three days . . . which seems short, but the total number of hours and the trauma endured made it feel so much longer.

Within three weeks, my lawyers called me with the verdict. "I'm sorry, but we lost." The judge said he believed my story but thought I should have made different choices. How is it possible for those two sides to co-exist? If someone truly believed the pressure I'd been under, they'd know I wasn't in the right headspace to make the decisions I would make in hindsight. It's easy to sit in a safe environment and look at an entire situation after the fact and say "That seems a bit off." I think it seems off as well! But they weren't in my situation; they weren't exposed to the grooming and manipulation that I was exposed to.

I had the option to take the case to a higher court. With what money I had left, I told my lawyers yes, I wanted to go for another round. There were several things I could have done differently; I didn't have a psychologist speak on my behalf, for example. And the law I was trying to use was complex; there was a sentence in the law that we didn't prove properly. I wanted another chance.

It was now April 2020. The trial was to be held in August 2020, during the COVID-19 pandemic. I couldn't go home to my family, and my family couldn't be with me. I was busy working on my defense in court, at the same time I was working full time at my job. The perfect time, one bank decided, to contact debt collectors in the UK and start siccing them on me.

I couldn't also afford a lawyer in the UK. I couldn't fight in two countries. That was the start of my applying for bankruptcy in the UK. I started the process before I even went back on trial and had a verdict. I felt I had no choice. I had to do what I could to protect myself, because now it looked like they were going to try to take me to court in the UK, where I lived and worked. I had a feeling the trial wasn't going to go the way I wanted it to go, and I just wanted to stop the suffering.

The staff at the Insolvency Registry (which handles bankruptcy cases) were really kind to me when I filed for bankruptcy. The punishment is the bankruptcy itself, was their philosophy. They didn't want to put me through further suffering. They looked at all the debt I had—including my debt in Norway—and the money I had coming in through my job, and established a budget for me, with a monthly sum I had to pay to my creditors. Someone with a low salary would need to pay nothing; I ended up having to pay about $250 per month, which left me enough to live on without having to feel like I wasn't living at all. Still, it was not a pleasant experience to go through. When you file for bankruptcy, your bank accounts get shut down; you don't have access to the money you make. Imagine the stress of not having a bank card in today's world. To be able to function, I opened an account with an online bank.

All this was right before the second trial in Norway. This trial was different, because of COVID-19. Only my parents were there for support. My best friend was there, too, but not to testify for me this time. The bank's legal team wanted her to testify against me! She had no choice but to take the stand. They wanted to prove that I wasn't in a dire situation because when I met up with my friend during that time, I didn't tell her what I was going through, and I had seemed normal. They were trying to destroy my character, to argue that I was lying in court. If they understood the crime, they would have known I'd been coerced by Simon to not say anything to anyone about what I was going through. Besides, as my friend testified, when we saw each other, we were in a group setting; I wouldn't have shared something that personal in that type of situation.

I also had a psychologist testify, one whom I'd hired to interview me in advance and write a report. What was so difficult to explain in court was why I didn't have "written proof" of some of the emotional tactics Simon used on me. Some evidence could be found in the text messages and voice notes in WhatsApp, but there was so much more that we talked about on a regular phone call or FaceTime call, which is not recorded. I could hear the distress in Simon's voice and the pressure he put on me, but the court kept insisting, "It's not in written form." Ironic, how when it's to the bank's advantage to accept a loan application, they don't require "written proof" of much.

The representative from the bank that forgave my debt testified for me as well. The banks' lawyers tried to make it sound like he hadn't done his job properly. During the break, he said to my mom, "I have no idea why they're doing this. We have insurance for this."

The banks' lawyers said in court, "It's very tragic that Cecilie was defrauded, but it's not the bank's fault." They'd rather go after me than Simon, because I was the weak one. I couldn't even go after my criminal myself, because the police were treating me like a suspect at that point, and I didn't have the money to file a big lawsuit against him (thankfully, the banks didn't know I was being looked at as a suspect, or they most certainly would have tried to use that to their advantage).

I thought for a bit that the judges were on our side. One of the lawyers on the banks' side argued, "You can't say there were threats when they weren't real" (since Simon was lying about the security threats). The judge replied, "But what if someone came up to you and said, 'I have a gun' and held their hand under their shirt in the shape of a gun. Was there a threat? You believe that there was."

But in the end, I lost that trial, too.

I felt like a puppet in a big system. The courts are often bound by previous verdicts and the existing laws (which are not brought up to date for the digital world). When other court cases have been massively ruled in favor of the banks, it's almost impossible to win. Even if I had won that trial, the banks would have taken the case to an even higher court, and I didn't have enough money to fight back again. It feels impossible as an individual to go up against large powerful banks with billions of dollars in surplus each year—four of them, at that!

My case is a microcosm of how society views fraud as a whole: we blame the victims. It's not just fraud, either. Society sometimes blames victims of rape, too. The court system tells you that you could have avoided the situation, you could have dressed differently, you could have said *NO* louder, you could have told someone sooner, and it's your fault. Misogynistic, a bit? It's the same with relationship fraud.

There are no laws that protect fraud victims in these situations, especially back in 2020 in Norway. At that time, there was nothing I could do. Even though the judges believed my story, there were no laws they could apply that would allow me to win. It's rather a Catch-22 situation; until more relationship fraud victims go to court, there aren't enough precedents to use as examples and to instigate changes in laws.

So where are things for me now? I can say that filing for bankruptcy in the UK saved me. I do still, however, have poor credit as a result of it (the bankruptcy remains on my file for six years), which makes it difficult for me to rent a flat, and I can't get a credit card or buy anything on credit. But it gave me some breathing space and protection, so I am forever grateful.

My loans in Norway continue to accrue with interest; I think they're collectively up to $300,000 now. I reached out to my creditors twice, first through my bankruptcy that they refused to accept, and another time offering to have a meeting to negotiate a percentage that I could pay. They used that opportunity to suggest that I take out more loans to pay them back. I am still contacted annually by my creditors: *Don't forget, you still owe us money.*

I'm still so deflated and sad over the reality of my situation, but I can't let it keep me from moving forward. If I wanted to move back to Norway, I would immediately have to file for bankruptcy there. According to Norway's process, I would have to work my butt off for five to seven years, giving everything but the bare minimum of my income that I was allowed to live off to these giant banks that treated me like I was worthless. After that time period, the remaining debt would be forgiven, but why would I want to suffer for so long, when it was not even me that committed the crime? Norway's system favors the banks; you are barely allowed to survive.

The bankruptcy system in the UK is much more consumer friendly; they regulate the monthly payments to allow you to live a decent life and forgive any remaining debt after three years. They want you to be able to rebuild your life sooner.

Trolls who don't know me say that I haven't taken any responsibility for my actions, since I filed for bankruptcy in the UK and have not paid back the Norwegian loans. Believe me, I've taken hard hits. I've destroyed so much of my future. I lost my flat in Norway. I lost the money from the sale of my flat by having to defend myself in court. I had to file for bankruptcy, which I'm still feeling the effects of today. All of these are traumatic incidents in someone's life, and that's only in respect to the financial side of what I've been through. How long is it okay for me to suffer?

Still, I'm more fortunate than many fraud victims; I have emotional support from my family (and I had my mother to handle communication with the banks early on, when I was too traumatized to handle that myself). Not everyone does. I also had the ability to hire lawyers (in Norway, there is no right to legal representation). When I think of those people who had a serious crime committed against them and did not survive the banks' relentless hunt for money in the aftermath, my heart breaks. Some banks refuse to acknowledge that they can kill people with their policies. It's not only the devastation of losing control over our finances that we face; we lose any sense of security over our lives. Our futures don't feel like ours to build anymore.

I'm grateful that I'm more angry than sad at this point. I had enough good cries over it all. I'm rechanneling that emotion into fighting with everything I have to expose the systemic failures that have existed for years. I want to be a thorn in their side. I wrote an opinion piece for a newspaper; I've been active on Twitter/X and LinkedIn, tagging the banks with my posts and comments. Not surprisingly, I have not spoken to any of the larger banks in Norway, nor have I been invited to speak at any of their financial conferences. However, abroad my expertise and experience are welcomed, and it's amazing being able to share and highlight the human side of fraud.

At least the UK government is doing an inquiry into fraud. In the UK, I'm contacted every Valentine's Day by media eager to share stories about the dangers of romance fraud—a crucial and impactful way to raise awareness. But in Norway, there's been silence. The banks have downplayed the significance of fraud, trying to act as if it's not a serious issue in society. They've failed to stand on the right side of history, despite the growing prevalence of this kind of crime.

Recently, however, I've noticed a shift in Norway; the conversation is beginning to change. It's remarkable how much time it took. In 2024, fraud was finally labeled a societal problem by the Economic Crime Unit in Norway (ØkoKrim). One of the top executives of Norway Finance (an umbrella organization for banks in Norway) recently stated that we all need to unite against the real criminals. While I'm surprised and encouraged by this, it's a stark contrast to their usual approach—making fraud victims bear full responsibility, even putting them on trial for crimes committed against them.

I am happy these Norwegian entities are starting to come around, and I welcome them to join forces with the banks in the UK. Collaboration is the key. A lot of hardworking banking employees are wanting to do right by their consumers and do more for victims, and I know that theirs is not an easy position to be in. I just wish for more humanity and empathy in financial cases, and it looks like we're headed there. This fight is a marathon, not a sprint.

Pernilla

Credit card companies, such as American Express, track their customers' spending patterns. If someone typically spends $1,000 or $2,000 a month, then suddenly charges $6,000 or $7,000, it will flag their system and stop the card. At the time I was being defrauded by Simon, I was using my American Express card to cover my daily spending and travel expenses, which came to several thousand dollars per month. Spending $6,000 or so on flights for Simon wouldn't have set off an alarm bell with the company; it was not unusual spending for me. Besides, I had a history of always paying my bills on time, so they had no cause for concern.

However, there's another reason AMEX should have contacted me. They had known about Simon being a fraudster for months . . . years. Not only were tickets being purchased in his name on my card, but my name had been on Cecilie's AMEX credit card statements months ago. They knew how Simon operated; it was a Ponzi scheme—he used one woman's credit card to wine and dine the next victim. They knew I was next in line to be defrauded, and they did nothing to stop it.

When I learned that Simon was a fraudster, I got in contact with AMEX's security department because I was furious with them. How dare they tell Cecilie not to contact me? Sure, they were working on their investigation, but aren't they supposed to protect their customers? I had been a Platinum AMEX customer for around ten years; Sweden and the UK share customer service data—they knew this. How could they treat their customers this way? The only response I got back was that "a mistake was made at work." *What does that even mean? And what are you going to do to rectify it?*

Again, they did nothing. I tried to recoup the money Simon had charged to my AMEX card, but because I'd already paid the bill, I was told they couldn't refund me. I felt I was being punished for having done the right thing by paying my bill. Since it was too late to dispute the bill, I was told I'd have to take them to court. I had limited energy and resources. I had to pick my battles . . . there were so many to choose from.

I was also furious at my Swedish bank for erroneously telling me that the transfer Simon had sent me was legitimate, and that the money should arrive in my account soon. When I questioned them about that in the aftermath, they said, "We don't know if an employee actually said that. Do you have it in writing?" Of course I didn't have it in writing—I had shown up to the bank in person!

I also wanted to file a lawsuit against the bank in the Netherlands for accepting my transfer for Simon through Joan, his supposed employee at LLD Diamonds. Joan's account had already been under fraudulent alert; when I submitted the transfer, I was supposed to have been notified of this—or at least my Swedish bank should have been notified. But I never received any notice.

But taking a large bank to court as a private person proved extremely difficult. No Swedish lawyer wanted to take on the case. I called around seventy law firms in Sweden, and they all said no. I was so frustrated! Through a friend, I was given the phone number of a lawyer who gave me insight into my dilemma, confidentially. Because all the large law firms used or had relationships with Sweden's largest bank—the one I wanted to take on—they feared burning bridges with a powerful institution. The banks, therefore, knew they could get away with whatever they wanted.

The lawyer recommended that I hire a lawyer in the Netherlands, who didn't have the same conflict of interest. I spent somewhere between $15,000 and $20,000 to take that bank to court. Naïvely, I was so sure I'd win. But I lost. They argued that the person who accepted the money—Joan—was also a victim, not the fraudster. Perhaps that was initially true, but she had become an accomplice, so she was a fraudster, too! Anyway, I wasn't taking her to court (although I wanted to); I was contesting the way the bank mishandled the transaction. Ironically, the bank must have spent more money defending itself against me than they would have if they had just refunded me the thirty-two thousand euros I had transferred to Joan's account. But I felt they wanted to use my case as an example to other fraud victims: *If you try to come after us, you will fail.*

Not only did I lose about $50,000 to Simon, I lost another several thousand to legal fees that I am still making monthly payments toward, since I'd had to take out a loan. I do take personal responsibility for having made a very bad decision in trusting the person that I did. Still, I am adamant that those people and institutions that could have stopped the scam but didn't should also be held accountable. They have a responsibility toward their clients that they're not fulfilling. They use their position of power to scare people off from challenging them, which means they can continue to take advantage of us.

There's so much more I would have liked to do in my fight for justice. But it was all too much to handle at once. As victims, we have to prioritize where to put our energy. It's good to fight, but it's also good to know our limits. In the end, I put more effort into trying to get Simon arrested than I did trying to get my money back.

Before this all happened, I had a lot more trust in banks. But after going through everything I did, I realize what a dirty business it is. In Sweden, we need to change the system to allow for checks and balances and more regulations in the banking system; it should be easier to hire lawyers in the country to go after banks, without presenting a conflict of interest. Banks should have procedures that prevent the approval of $50,000 transactions to Nigeria, for example. International transactions should take longer to process, so there is time to detect fraud.

My faith in the justice system is severely lacking, too. In Sweden, cases are decided by a single judge, who only has the laws as they are currently written to work with. Even if they personally feel that someone is guilty and they wish to convict them, if the law doesn't align with that judgment, they cannot. And current laws are outdated; laws in Sweden seem to be changing somewhat in regard to fraud, but we're still far away from where we need to be. We need to put more pressure on banks to implement systems that reduce fraud; there are now technologies that detect fraudulent behavior much earlier on that many banks aren't using. Maybe they don't think fraud impacts their business enough to warrant the change, but in time, it will. The scam industry is just continuing to grow.

There is a false perception among the public that if we are defrauded, we will get our money back. Either the bank will refund the money, or some other entity will (some people think homeowner's/renter's insurance or some other type of insurance will take care of it). If I was robbed, for example, insurance probably would cover the loss. If someone held a gun to my head and made me withdraw money at an ATM, the bank would probably give me that money back. I received death threats from Simon, but he never held a gun on me . . . to the police, banks, insurance, and justice systems, there seems to be a difference.

Once money leaves your bank through relationship or confidence fraud, it's a dirty road ahead. When you're already under mental duress from having been defrauded, the impact of the aftermath can be even more devastating than the financial loss itself. My heart breaks when I read about older people, especially, who have lost their life savings to fraud; at least I am young enough that I have time to try to rebuild my life. What is an elderly person, without the ability to work, supposed to do? I can't imagine that feeling of hopelessness. Whatever I can do to help prevent people from getting into that situation, I am determined to do.

EDUCATING FINANCIAL INSTITUTIONS

Fraud education is not prioritized with the police, and with financial institutions we've sometimes seen the same. Most bank employees probably don't even know what relationship fraud truly is. Many of the conferences we speak at are for tech businesses, which focus on statistics. The lightbulbs go on when they hear our personal stories and realize we are not just a data point or a line in an Excel spreadsheet. Education involves explaining what the crime truly is with research and showing how pervasive it is with numbers, but then backing those numbers up with the human side.

When it comes to bank employees, how do we train them to recognize when a consumer is being scammed, and then how to handle the situation? There's no golden answer for this, because everyone has their own unique story. However, we can move toward a best practice. In the direst of cases, it's not enough to call the consumer and simply say "We have some questions about the use of your card" or "We know you're not the one using your card." Think about it—why would someone lend out their card to someone they know in the first place? Most likely, there is some sort of emotional manipulation going on. Banks need to think differently about their processes when it comes to fraud; perhaps they need a specialized team when it comes to the more intricate cases, when victims refuse to believe they're being defrauded. The first-line employee is probably not well enough trained to effectively handle those kinds of conversations.

Although each case is unique, some processes can be streamlined. Currently, each bank is allowed to come to their own conclusion regarding whether a consumer's debt should be forgiven. Some banks contact the police when they notice signs of fraud; some just let the transfer go through. Some banks call the victim several times to try to make them understand they are being defrauded, but they never get through, or they get yelled at by the consumer who is not ready to accept that they're being defrauded. (Either way, as we'll discuss in an upcoming chapter, the more friction, the better. It shouldn't be so easy to take out high-interest loans or lend our cards to someone else.)

Protocols could be put in place regarding how to handle fraud victims. Various red flags could signal certain procedures. If a bank notices a lot of transactions to other banks or several loans being taken out, or if Experian notices a high volume of credit checks in a short period of time, they could initiate a health check on that person. If someone takes those actions, they're not in a good headspace.

Banks communicating with one another is particularly important in fraud cases, since it's likely that fraud victims are having to pull funds and request loans from multiple banks to meet the demands of the fraudster. Banks could collaborate with each other; if a bank gets a notion that someone is being defrauded—for example, they see multiple transfers to another bank—they could efficiently notify the receiving bank that they've seen warning signs that this person is being defrauded. We'd like to see more communication among banks and, more importantly, for banks to not view fraud as a business. There are no "business secrets" when it comes to fraud. There should be best practices, built around fraud prevention and protecting their customers. If a bank has established a best practice to approach fraud victims (without victim blaming), for example, they should share that with other banks. That is not happening today. If banks helped each other in today's world of globalization, they'd all be less likely to be taken down by the growing fraud industry.

WHY MOST FRAUD VICTIMS ARE SCREWED . . . FOR NOW

The sad reality is that most victims of relationship fraud will never get their money back or their debts cleared. Perhaps that will change . . . we're certainly trying to work toward that effect. We feel our best shot is to keep attention focused on this issue and the pressure on. The UK has already come a long way since we were defrauded.

The key is to understand what happened to you, so that you know what you need to apply for, and you need to fight—no bank will ever willingly refund you. Even if the bank comes back and says, "No, we're not going to refund you," don't take no for an answer. Often victims are not strong enough to do this, which is what the banks are relying on. They want you to move on and forget it ever happened to you.

What makes relationship fraud particularly challenging is that our criminals use our names and our hands to make transactions, so their hands look clean. They are professional criminals; they know how to use social engineering to make us do what they want, and how to use police and banking processes to their advantage. They even know which banks to target. Plus, most of the transactions are made online, so they aren't even in the same country as the victim and their bank (or local law enforcement).

For most fraud victims to get their money back, and in this day and age of globalization and easy access to foreign payment processors, we need stronger international police and for banks to collaborate across countries. We also need banks to understand that refunding victims of fraud will not cause the number of fraud cases to rise. An argument banks like to make to avoid giving refunds is that people will take more purchasing risks. TSB Bank in England introduced their "Fraud Refund Guarantee" in 2019, a break from the rest of the banking sector, and pledged to refund all innocent victims of fraud at a time when the industry refund rate was just 19%. Since then, TSB have refunded 97% of all customers who have fallen victim to act fraud. "[TSB hasn't] seen an uptick either in [their] customers taking less care or making more claims."*

That's because nobody wants to be a victim of fraud. When consumers are at the point of making payments, they are not thinking about being scammed. If they were, they probably wouldn't make the payment. But all this research falls on deaf ears.

Some banks try to instill fear in the public by saying, "If we forgive the debt, it will be more expensive for you." We know that's false. They're trying to pit the people on the bottom—consumers and fraud victims—against each other, while those at the top continue collecting their billions.

The system is indeed challenging, with powerful forces like the police, banks, and the justice system on one side, and a single victim on the other. They understand the intricacies of the system in ways we may not. But we've also met countless dedicated bank employees and police officers who genuinely wish they could do more. They're not unempathetic or complacent; they're simply caught in the overwhelming rise of fraud cases that flood their daily work.

HOT TIPS

- An FTC report revealed cryptocurrency and bank wires as the most common methods of how romance scammers take money; together, they accounted for more than 60 percent of reported losses to romance scams in 2022. Gift cards is another commonly used method to scam romance fraud victims. Here's a tip: Nobody legit will ever ask you to help (or insist that you invest) by sending cryptocurrency,

---

* https://committees.parliament.uk/oralevidence/14233/pdf/

giving the numbers on a gift card, or wiring money. Anyone who does is a scammer.*

- If you've been defrauded, don't take *no* for an answer when a bank tells you they won't refund you the money.

- Keep a paper trail of every communication you have with your bank; record phone calls and ask for written statements even when you show up in person.

---

* U.S. Federal Trade Commission, Data Spotlight, "Romance Scammers' Favorite Lies Exposed," February 9, 2023, https://www.ftc.gov/news-events/data-visualizations/data-spotlight/2023/02/romance-scammers-favorite-lies-exposed#ft9.

CHAPTER 8

The Media

~~Why did you make him famous?~~
~~Why do we only care about what drives clicks?~~

The *Tinder Swindler* documentary, released in February 2022, became Netflix's second most viewed documentary . . . ever (it was ousted by Prince Harry and Meghan Markle's docuseries, which came out in December 2022). It was nominated for five Emmy Awards, including Outstanding Documentary or Nonfiction Special. It won the 2023 Royal Television Society (RTS) Television Award for Best Single Documentary. The accolades are nice, but what we're more excited about and proud of is the fact that the film gave victims a voice.

The role of the press is critical. Without the press, no one would have believed our story. The work the journalists at *VG* did to show that Simon can be caught and the questions they asked helped get us some answers. By going public with our story through the biggest streaming service in the world, we got Simon's face out there and saved countless people from getting scammed. The power of that is immense.

Then there's the other side. The language used in some media stories is very judgmental and places blame on the victim (for example, we "fell" for a scam or were "duped").

Headlines are written to drive clicks, at the cost of victims' livelihoods. Our trauma was turned into true crime entertainment, and Simon's role as a criminal was glorified.

In some ways, we feel we became the bad guys while the real bad guys roam free.

Cecilie

When I decided to go public with my story, I knew I had to reach out to Norway's most-read newspaper—*VG*. In mid-June 2018, I submitted a tip through their website and very quickly received a response that my story sounded interesting, and they'd like to schedule a follow-up call. *Finally!* I felt so relieved. *Someone else is as shocked by what I've been through as I am!* I'd taken so many blows from the police and banks that even if all this amounted to was a phone call, someone at least thought what I had to say was worth investigating.

First, we had a fairly short call to answer some basic questions about the case. "I have the entire WhatsApp chat I had with Simon. Do you want it?" I asked. The journalist later told me that that's very rare; for privacy's sake, most people send screenshots of selected excerpts or at least delete photos or videos exchanged (these are romantic relationships, after all!), but I didn't care. I wanted them to understand the entire picture of what I'd been through. Plus, I didn't have the time or energy to filter through months' worth of daily messages. I sent them everything.

Then I waited. It was summer vacation time in Norway. They didn't start working properly on the piece in earnest until August. One of the first steps they took was to attempt to properly ID Simon, which they did by flying to Tel Aviv, finding his mother's apartment (where he was receiving mail) and his mother, and speaking with Israeli law enforcement about prior charges against him, along with finding the court documents from his Finnish case.

They were investigative journalists; they didn't just want to tell a sensationalized story, they wanted to reveal new details about the case. In Norway, we call the media the guard dog of right and wrong in society. If the people in power who are supposed to protect and inform us fail to do so, at least we have another avenue to pursue in an effort to achieve justice. The media served that purpose for me.

After a long period of silence, things started happening, very quickly. In January 2019, I was at work when I received a call from *VG* that they'd found another victim who wanted to come forward (Pernilla); they were on their way to Munich to film her meeting up with Simon. The relief I felt was palpable. Although I wasn't allowed to contact the other victim until after the piece was published, a huge weight was lifted from my shoulders. I was so scared to come out with my story, but now I wasn't going to be doing it alone. By the end of February 2019, *VG* released an incredible digital documentary that, although it didn't go into great depth, told a powerful story—one that instantly went viral.

When I finally got to meet Pernilla, it was like meeting someone I'd known forever. I knew her energy; we are so similar. It was healing for me to hear that she understood why I had dated Simon; he'd truly seemed like a good-hearted person and was funny and lovable. She made me realize how calculated and good he was at his "job." Now it was time for us to go to work. Pernilla has the same fighting spirit as I do, and we had a shared goal: *Let's get Simon!*

Pernilla

I was extremely nervous when the *VG* article was about to come out. I knew that I was going to be judged. I'd never seen an article about a fraud victim who was painted in a positive light—especially not a woman. Often, victims' faces are blurred in media stories to protect their identities. But I knew I had to show my face to give our story the best chance at being heard—and make Simon and his accomplices more likely to be caught. Knowing that another victim, whom I hadn't yet met, was also coming forward and showing her face made it easier to be brave enough to do the same.

The day the article was posted, my phone blew up with calls and text messages from friends, family, and colleagues. I didn't have the energy to talk to anyone that day; I spent most of the day lying in bed, feeling sick with nerves. There was one person I felt motivated to talk to, however. The one person who truly understood what I was feeling.

Cecilie reached out to me through social media. Over the next few days, we commiserated together over the phone for hours and hours and made plans to meet up in London, where we were scheduled to do an interview with an Israeli TV news station. When we finally met in person, we shared the best hug I have had in my entire life, to this day. We had already become so close; she was the only person I could confide in so openly, whom I didn't have to explain anything to and who didn't judge me, since she had been through the same thing. Then, only about forty-five minutes after we met, we held our first interview together. When the journalist asked each question, we looked at each other, knowing we were both thinking the same thing. Our connection is telepathic; we're more than best friends, we are like sisters.

After the interview, we immediately went to work, sending the *VG* article to every news outlet we could find. It spread like wildfire. Our constant pushing didn't end when we left each other's side in London. Over the course of the next six months, message by message, phone call by phone call, interview by interview, we created our own media storm, contacting and talking to any outlet that would listen to our story—so long as they showed Simon's face. If the police, the financial institutions, and the governments weren't going to do anything, we would. We made ourselves available to anyone who would let us expose Simon and educate them on the horrible experiences fraud victims endure, something we were still very much in the throes of ourselves.

That's what's crazy: we were still living the story. I hadn't had any time to process all the trauma. From first being contacted by *VG* to finding out I'd lost everything, flying to Munich, and then flying to London to meet with Cecilie, only about eight weeks had passed. I was still receiving death threats from Simon. I was so drained and mentally unstable. Now, on top of everything, we were also trying to learn the media industry. I was so fragile back then that I could not have handled it all by myself. Having Cecilie beside me made the media storm endurable. Some of the articles being written about us were so judgmental and hateful, not to mention some of the comments being made online. I understand how people can become suicidal, based on that factor alone. At the same time, having people to talk to about what had happened to me was therapy, in a way. Fighting back against my fraudster gave me purpose; it was something to focus on, rather than just the fear and pain.

I hadn't talked much with my friends about what had happened to me leading up to the *VG* piece, because I hadn't had time. I had called my dad first to explain what had happened with Simon and told him he had to call my mom and tell her, because it was too hard for me to explain it all over again. The rest of my family and friends learned about it through the *VG* article.

I lost some friends after going public. I can't say that I'm disappointed in that, however, because the experience showed me who my true friends are. The ones who were in my life just because I had money were the first to fall out of my life. I heard co-workers talk about me behind my back, too. I walked into a room when one of them was saying, "I can't believe she did that, I would never do that." I wanted to say no one ever knows what they'd do in that situation until they're in it. But I didn't have energy to put toward that fight. Nor did I have the time. Everything was happening so fast.

Within a few weeks of the release of the *VG* documentary, several U.S. film and TV agents reached out to *VG*, asking who owned the life rights to our story. Fortunately, we did. After meeting with several agents, we felt most aligned with Addison Duffy from United Talent Agency and by March, we had a deal. She sold our story to AGC Studios, which now owns our life rights in documentary and film. AGC chose Raw TV in England to film what would become our documentary, *The Tinder Swindler*, with Netflix contracted for distribution.

When we had the meeting with AGC Studios, we knew they were the ones we trusted with our most personal, sensitive story. Director Felicity Morris, producer Bernadette Higgins, and everyone else on the RAW TV team were professional and phenomenal people. Their jobs were made extra complicated because filming took place in December 2020, during the COVID-19 pandemic, when everything was shut down. Fortunately, Sweden opened the borders long enough for them to fly from the UK to meet with me for eighteen hours straight. They were in town for two or three days, but all my interviews took place in one day.

Again, I still hadn't mentally processed all of what had happened to me yet; there I was, sitting for interviews, on camera, surrounded by enthusiastic and creative people, while reliving my deepest trauma in a language that wasn't even my own. I was so tired. And so scared. How was the film going to turn out? Was what I was saying making any sense?

When the film was finished, Cecilie and I were invited to a preview screening. We were so anxious. Felicity and Bernadette tried to calm us down. "You have to trust us," they said.

"We don't trust anyone," we said, with nervous laughter. But we watched the film and agreed: It was amazing.

Cecilie

My experience making *The Tinder Swindler* began with countless video calls to create an outline for when we filmed in person. Then we had two days to record my story in London in November 2020. A cozy restaurant in East London was rented for the shoot; the concept was to film me as if I were telling my story to someone while on a date. Pandemic circumstances made the shoot more difficult; we had to wear masks when we weren't actively filming, socially distance, and have all the doors open (it was freezing!).

What was further challenging was that I had to tell my story in real time, as if it were happening in present day. I had to relive a wide range of emotions in a very short time—falling in love, sadness, anger, resentment, and even wanting to die. I'm not an actress, so every emotion I expressed was real. I wanted people to see the hurt that Simon caused me, and I feel I was able to convey that, thanks to the entire team at Raw TV that made me feel comfortable. I couldn't have worked with a better director or producer; they showed me so much love and took such great care of my story.

Because we were condensing a real-life story spanning several months into a ninety-minute film, the timeline was adapted and compressed, but that didn't take away from the heart of my story. I stand by what I said in the film about love; despite what I've been through, I still believe in the perfect love. What is wrong with wanting or wishing for that? I'm proud that I had the courage to be honest and real in front of the cameras and let go of control over what happened next.

We had no contact with Netflix before the film came out in February 2022, but we knew from working with Raw TV that a lot of resources were being put into the documentary to make it look great. Once the film came out, it spread far more quickly than the *VG* piece. With online streaming, our story became available worldwide, all at once. Subtitles were available in many different languages, in addition to dubbing (it is hilarious to hear voices in different languages come out of our mouths on screen!).

We've been through two global press tours, the first after *VG*'s piece came out, and the second after the release of the Netflix documentary, which was an all-out media storm. We were on TV shows such as *Dr. Phil, The Drew Barrymore Show, Tamron Hall,* ABC's *Nightline, Entertainment Tonight, Inside Edition, CBS Mornings,* and many more. Our story was featured in *The New York Times, The Times UK, Forbes, British Vogue, Cosmopolitan, GQ, People,* and countless more publications worldwide.

By then, I'd already experienced many pros and cons of being in the media. For one thing, I'd learned how little control we have over the narrative—what was being said about us or shared online. Not long after the *VG* piece came out, *The Daily Mail* in the UK reached out to me, asking if they could use my social media photos with an article they were publishing on our story. I wasn't given a chance to respond, however, before they went ahead and used them. I was upset at the time, but when I think now about the number of photos of me online that have been used without my permission, that's not where I want to channel my energy.

Nor do I want to put it toward reading comments. Initially, I was logging on to social media and not only reading some of the horrendous comments but responding to them. Big mistake. "I don't think you would have dared to say that to my face!" I replied to one commenter who was especially brutal. I was so angry about the cruel things people were saying about me, but more than that, I worried that exposing ourselves in this way wasn't going to have the effect we'd wanted. Were people going to take romance fraud seriously? Was it going to make any sort of dent in how financial institutions and law enforcement entities handle this type of crime? Were any tech companies or institutions—or Simon and his accomplices—going to be held accountable? I felt they were all getting off too easily.

I understand better now why it's so difficult to hold powerful institutions' feet to the fire. If a journalist sends questions to a bank, for example, they most likely won't even reply. They're only likely to apply pressure for a response if the public demands it. But the public doesn't really care (until they get defrauded themselves). Some commenters referenced a need for these entities to be held at least somewhat responsible, but many others (who in my opinion didn't understand the crime) instead blamed us. Without public consensus that there is more to this story worth pursuing, journalists will quickly move on to other stories.

After the *VG* piece, several more articles did come out, featuring additional victims of Simon's. But after the Netflix documentary was released, no major media outlet underwent further investigative work. Netflix put in an amazing effort; they created a podcast series that revealed further information about Simon, other victims and accomplices, and the psychology behind the crime. But how many people have heard that podcast compared to the number of people who have seen *The Tinder Swindler*? The biggest disappointment for me is that the documentary has been looked upon by some of the public—and much of the media—as pure entertainment. But no wonder; we as a society love true crime, myself included.

There's a duality about going public with a crime; on one hand, it stops the perpetrator from being able to continue with their crime. Simon's reign is over in that sense; he might be able to defraud more people since he's not in jail, but his face and his crime have been exposed, which makes it much more difficult. On the other hand, victims become extremely vulnerable.

For example, I learned so much about how words can be twisted in an effort to drive clicks. Because I'd already gone public, the banks' legal case against me was filmed in court and covered by the media. While on the stand, I was asked if I would do what I'd done for Simon again if I were placed in that situation again today. I said yes—if I believed I could protect someone I loved, I would do it again today. If I had said no, I would have lost my case automatically. It was a difficult position to be in; statements given in court, with the media present, can easily be taken out of context and left for the journalist to decide how they want to interpret and represent those words. Some chose to twist my words and make it sound like I'd said I would willingly allow myself to be defrauded again.

Another journalist twisted my words about my reaction to the Netflix documentary. I said in the interview that I'd had to say a lot of private things that I didn't want to say. I mean, who really wants to say how many years they've been single, how many dates they've been on, or if they have sex on the first date, knowing that those answers will be broadcast for a global audience? But the journalist framed my comment as if I'd said the film producers had forced me to say things I didn't want to say, which was not at all the truth. I answered every question willingly, because I understood we needed those answers for viewers to understand who I am as a person.

That's the conflict with using true crime as entertainment. Going public with my story has changed my life. I'm eternally grateful for all the good that has come from having been given the opportunity to expose my criminal. Many victims aren't so fortunate. But true crime is based on the premise of taking someone's vulnerability and trauma and broadcasting it for people to twist and judge, as a distraction from daily life. I have no regrets and am truly proud of my contribution toward both the *VG* piece and the Netflix documentary. But I'm also allowed to mourn a bit for the loss of my privacy and the use of my trauma for entertainment as opposed to education.

One aspect of being in the media is the public reaction; another is the reaction of family, friends, and colleagues. I am extremely fortunate to have had the unconditional support of my family throughout this entire journey. I don't know what I would have done without them. I was also blessed to have had an incredibly supportive work environment; in the beginning, when my world flipped upside down, I could go to work and be reminded that the crime I'd endured wasn't my entire life. Like Pernilla, I did lose some relationships during that time, but the friends I have now are my ride-or-dies. They are so supportive and proud of me. "Think about where you are now, compared to back then," they remind me when I'm feeling down.

Then there are my public talks. I belong to a speaker talent agency in Norway, and after the Netflix documentary came out, the agency received a call from a woman who was appalled that they would represent "someone like me." She didn't think I was worthy of having a voice because she thought the crime was my fault (victim blaming 101). The agency stood by me. At my talks, the audience response is overwhelmingly positive; most of the talks I give are within the fraud space, so they understand the crime. What I offer is the human side to the numbers. Personal stories are more impactful than looking at victim statistics on a spreadsheet. I tell my audiences, however, that I want them to ask critical questions, if they have them. If they are thinking, "Why didn't you do X, Y, or Z?" I want to be able to answer that question, from a psychological or logistical standpoint. That's the only way to reverse the stigma—through education.

One of the best things about going public is that other victims of relationship fraud feel less alone. We receive messages all the time. "I was defrauded. Can you help me tell my story?" There are so many others who want to go public now, because they, too, want their fraudster's face out there. People are also more aware of the crime now, so they're looking for red flags and taking fewer risks. I didn't know this type of crime existed when I got defrauded—I'd never been exposed to people who could be so evil. But now, people know.

I don't think I've fully come to terms yet with how big the *Tinder Swindler* documentary has become, and how fortunate we are to have the platform that we have. Most victims don't have that. *Tinder swindled* is now a verb (for example, "I almost got Tinder swindled"). Actress Marisha Wallace bravely came forward in 2024 with her incredible story about being scammed by "The Bumble Swindler." Swindlers are everywhere. Relationship fraud is a global, multi-billion-dollar business. Thanks to the media, the public is more aware of this now and taking steps to protect themselves.

"CELEBRITY" CRIMINALS

People are highly fascinated with people who do things the average person could—or would—never do. Even though *The Tinder Swindler* was made with us victims at the forefront, as opposed to many true crime stories that place the criminal at the forefront, when true crime is used as entertainment, criminals become celebrities. At the end of the film, viewers see a man who has destroyed the lives of so many victims continuing to party it up as a free man. *How is that possible?* they wonder, wanting more.

We get it. We're fascinated by it, too. We've never seen someone who could do so many evil things, seemingly with no consequences. The danger, however, is that some people end up admiring him, or even wanting to be him. Savvy criminals capitalize off that fascination. Cameo, for example, is a social media platform where fans can pay their favorite "stars" to create personalized videos. Simon has been using the fact that he hasn't been convicted of a crime to earn money from "fans" through this platform. Cameo defended their decision to allow Simon to use their platform; they tweeted, "Cameo is standing firm about its decision," and said that the decision to partner with Leviev was heavily based on his metrics and following. Businesses just care about making money; from their perspective, Simon isn't hurting anyone by being on the platform—consumers are paying him voluntarily. Valid point, but what about his numerous victims? Isn't he hurting us? The personalized videos he makes use catchphrases from the film—from our trauma—for fun and entertainment. Where's the ethics in this situation? Why are criminals being enabled? Why does the public think the abuse we've undergone is funny? Here we are, trying to warn the public about a crime that causes a lot of harm, and this is how people behave? It shows the worst of society.

Even legit celebrities are part of the problem. American rapper Cardi B., for example, mocked Simon in a tweet: "My enemies are after me, please send me 100k." Moroccan American rapper French Montana posted a selfie of himself with Simon on a private plane, along with the caption "I can't believe I met the swindler." They have platforms they could be using to spread awareness about relationship fraud and the pain he's caused, but instead they use them to mock our trauma and brag about having met a criminal. This behavior adds fuel to the fire; Simon took advantage of more viral opportunities to build his own platform and make more money.

Some journalists invite Simon to give paid media interviews, treating the story as entertainment rather than an investigation into his crimes. They, too, are more fascinated by his fame than they are wanting answers. And of course, Simon lies in every interview, sometimes changing the story from interview to interview (the money we gave him was a loan between friends; he paid us back, and so on). Why aren't these journalists asking him for proof that it was "just a loan"? That he "paid us back"? When media hosts laugh alongside him and create rapport with him rather than ask tough questions, something is deeply wrong. These are not serious journalists, but sadly they are plentiful.

Other criminals featured in the media have profited off their newfound fame as well. Anna Delvey (real name Anna Sorokin)—a fraudster who posed as a wealthy heiress to access upper-class New York social and art scenes—had her crimes made into the Netflix series *Inventing Anna* and recently competed on *Dancing with the Stars*. Our culture considers a convicted felon a star. Even the government seems to be on board—Anna is on house arrest in New York, wearing an ankle monitor, and yet was given permission to travel to Los Angeles to compete on the show. Why is she being given special treatment? It's disgusting.

We don't want to make these people famous. That's not why we went public and made ourselves vulnerable. And we didn't make documentaries to make money, either. Many people have the preconceived notion that because we went public, our debts were cleared and we were made whole. Most people don't receive any payment for going public because we're not supposed to get paid for journalism. We have no intention to do anything but educate people so they don't become victims themselves, and to expose a criminal so that he can't continue with his crimes.

CLICKBAIT COMES AT A COST

A common media narrative has been to present Simon as someone who "seduced" women across Europe with his "luxurious lifestyle." We can both tell you, neither one of us felt seduced. He was charming, yes, but we felt we had genuine, loving relationships with him (and remember, he didn't act alone—he couldn't have done what he did by himself). The public, fueled by this media narrative, assumed that Simon spent a lot of money on us—treating us to expensive dinners, partying it up with us across Europe, and so on.

Nothing could be further from the truth. We've had to work so hard to try to make people understand that we were the milking cows, not Simon. Those videos shown in the documentary and elsewhere online of Simon out clubbing with Piotr, surrounded by beautiful women? We never saw those! But those are the "catchy" images and headlines that get people to click. Clickbait comes at a cost, however.

One of the most dangerous repercussions of this narrative is its contribution to the "incel" movement (short for "involuntary celibate"). Incel is the name of an online community of male supremacists who rage against women, blaming them for their sexless lives. They hate the female archetype they call "Stacys," who are obsessed with material goods and appearance and deny unattractive or awkward men their "right" to sex, in favor of attractive men with high financial or social status. This rhetoric doesn't simply remain in online commentary, however.

Incel-related violence against women has risen over the last several years and has been linked to more than 100 deaths and injuries since the first incel-inspired attack in 2014. In 2020, the Texas Department of Homeland Security urged law enforcement officers to "recognize incels as an emerging and dangerous terrorist threat, rather than merely a criminal threat." In 2022, the U.S. Secret Service warned that "hatred of women, and the gender-based violence that is associated with it, requires increased attention from everyone with a role in public safety."*

Unfortunately, our story has been used to fuel this movement. Cecilie took a bigger hit because her relationship with Simon was romantic. Headlines, many accompanied by a picture of Cecilie crying, refer to us as "gold-digging" women who got what we deserved. Videos have been uploaded, with podcast hosts explaining how our story proves female privilege and other incel ideology. The comments on these posts go further than calling us stupid or naïve women; they are enjoying seeing us struggle and cry. It's really, really dark.

We highlight some of the negative repercussions of going public because it's important to understand the stigma. But we don't take negative comments too hard, because they're bullshit. As advocates, however, we know these sentiments are out there, and other fraud victims who may not be strong enough to ignore them will read them. We don't want people to feel that these remarks are the consensus in society, because they're not. Since we established our own platforms,

---

* Rachael Fugardi, "Nine Years after Deadly 'Incel' Attack, Threat of Male Supremacism Is Growing," Southern Poverty Law Center, May 23, 2023, https://www.splcenter.org/news/2023/05/23/after-incel-attack-male-supremacism-growing.

the comments we have received have been overwhelmingly positive and supportive.

WHAT MEDIA MAKES POSSIBLE

Overall, we are deeply grateful for the role the media has played in our lives. Sharing our story has helped raise awareness about relationship fraud, educating others about the risks and warning signs and the manipulative and abusive nature of this crime (it's not just about money!). Going public has empowered other victims to come forward and seek help, knowing they are not alone.

Our criminal has been exposed; Simon has been banned from dating apps and many social media platforms. He can't continue with "business as usual," because his face has been plastered all over the world as a fraudster. Journalists have also shown law enforcement that Simon—and therefore other fraudsters—can be caught, and they give credibility to our stories.

We are using the platforms we now have not only to educate others but to encourage changes in policies, laws, and regulations that protect consumers and fraud victims. We've built careers out of going public; we have voices that people in law enforcement, banking, and technology are listening to.

Many victims have said to us that the police told them not to go public with the crimes against them, because it would ruin their investigation. It did ruin it for us, to some extent. But now that we know how few relationship fraud criminals get properly investigated and prosecuted, we feel we did the right thing. We feel we protected more people than we would have if we had waited for law enforcement to get something done themselves. Going to the media prevented us from feeling powerless. We took back some control.

HOT TIPS

- Focus on raising awareness and education, not sensationalizing crimes or glorifying criminals
- Research and trust credible journalists or platforms to share and consume stories responsibly
- Be cautious with your words—media can twist them, and headlines rarely tell the full story
- Avoid engaging with online comments; they often amplify negativity rather than foster understanding
- Respect the vulnerability and bravery of victims who share their stories publicly
- Prioritize empathy and mental health—whether you're a victim or a consumer of these stories

CHAPTER 9

The World Is Changing (and So Are We)

> ~~Would you do it all over again?~~
> *How do we make sure no one goes through this again?*

What we've been through is surreal. From being defrauded by someone we loved and trusted, to filming *The Tinder Swindler*, to serving as keynote speakers for law enforcement and banking officials and government politicians, it's an experience that's quite unbelievable, especially when you consider it's born from the absolute worst time of our lives.

Ultimately, as of this writing, we're still in life-disrupting debt, and Simon has still not been brought to task for his wrongs. And yet we're hopeful. We may not get justice in the ways we had first envisioned, but we are already getting justice in other ways. We now have platforms to educate others about the impacts of relationship fraud—a crime reported by over 64,000 victims in 2023 in the U.S. alone, with losses totaling $1.1 billion (and remember, only 15 percent of these crimes get reported!), that no one was talking about at the time we were defrauded.

Confidence fraud is one of the oldest crimes. We will never put an end to it entirely, because the methods criminals use to scam us are constantly evolving—especially now that technology is advancing at lightning speed. What we need to do is evolve with them. We can do this by educating law enforcement, financial institutions, governments, the media, and individuals, then getting all these players together to rally for change. There are more people fighting for good than there are people doing evil things, and history shows that, in the end, evil never wins.

This fight involves changing laws so that law enforcement is better equipped to protect victims and prosecute fraudsters; it involves holding banks and big tech accountable for their roles in allowing fraud to take place on their platforms; it involves changing the language used in media and society, away from victim blaming and toward victim empowerment. And finally, for us, the fight has involved changing ourselves. We are not just victims, we are survivors, with a new, shared purpose: leaving the world better than it was before we were defrauded.

CHANGES IN LEGISLATION

One of the reasons we remain hopeful? Positive changes are already happening in the legislative world. On October 7, 2024, new legislation went into effect in the UK that issues mandatory scam reimbursement rules, aiming to protect victims of authorized push payment (APP) fraud (where a fraudster tricks a victim into authorizing payments to an account controlled by the fraudster). This type of scam has become more prevalent with sophisticated AI and "deepfake" technology, accounting for £459 million lost to scammers in the UK in 2023 and prompting the debate: Who should bear responsibility for this type of fraud—the victims? The banks? The government?

In most cases, losses have been borne by the victims (and in some cases, their banks or payment service providers, but often only after lengthy legal processes). With this new law, payment service providers are required to reimburse victims of APP fraud up to £85,000 (subject to some "consumer standards of caution"—for example, how careful you were about protecting yourself before you sent the money).* Both sides of a transaction, the sender and receiver banks, are held equally responsible for the reimbursement, so neither can blame the other. This forces banks to be more mindful of the fraud ecosystem and ask additional questions before allowing money in or out of accounts.

This legislation is groundbreaking and has the global financial industry shaking; the United States and other countries are watching the UK to see what the potential fallout of this model may be. Will fraud increase? No research points in that direction, but it's one of the arguments banks are using to avoid responsibility. More likely, now that banks are taking a direct financial hit, they will actually do something about the problem itself, by implementing technology and procedures that prevent fraud in the first place.

When it comes to financial institutions taking responsibility, we'd rather use a carrot than a whip. But it seems that if they're not being whipped, they're not doing enough about this issue. They need to hurt financially; the stakeholders need to earn less money before they care. It doesn't matter if people kill themselves, or undergo foreclosure on their homes, or have mental health crises that place stress on the National Health Service, or on the public sector. At the end of the day, a bank is a business, which is why we need laws to protect us, the individuals. Because—and we want to be clear here—we don't want it to happen in the first place.

It is our hope that more countries will follow the UK's stance and place more responsibility on financial institutions for fraud—but not only upon them. Tech companies need to share the burden. If the scam started on Meta's platforms (Facebook, Instagram, WhatsApp, and so on) or on a dating app, they should contribute to victim reimbursement. Current legislation is missing bold callouts of tech companies' responsibility. Liz Ziegler, fraud prevention director

---

* Emma Allen and Andrew Spencer, "UK Introduces Mandatory Reimbursement Rules to Combat APP Fraud," TaylorWessing, October 15, 2024, https://www.taylorwessing.com/en/insights-and-events/insights/2024/10/dqr-uk-introduces-mandatory-reimbursement-rules-to-combat-app-fraud.

at Lloyds Banking Group, said in a statement on the bank's website: "Banks have been at the forefront of tackling the epidemic of scams, but they cannot fight it alone. It's high time tech companies stepped up to share responsibility for protecting their own customers. This means stopping scams at [the] source and contributing to refunds when their platforms are used to defraud innocent victims."*

Victims will continue to bear some of the loss, no matter what—if it's not financial, they'll still lose time and energy and experience some degree of emotional or mental trauma. But they shouldn't have to bear the entire burden. We're all part of this global issue. Fraud is conducted through a funnel: victims are targeted via a communication platform, then coerced into sending money through financial platforms. We need to make it more difficult for criminals to be able to use these platforms. But for tech companies to do anything about the problem, they also need to lose money.

Once again, the UK is leading this movement. The Online Safety Act, a new set of laws that protects children and adults online, was passed in October 2023. With this act, new responsibilities are placed on social media companies and search services that allow users to post content online or interact with each other, to prevent illegal activities on their platforms. Violators will be fined according to how many fake profiles they have on their platform and other ways in which they are not doing their due diligence to keep criminal activity off their platforms.

The act is certainly a step in the right direction, but overseeing it will undoubtedly be difficult; how many violators will actually be caught? How many will be brought to trial? With the power that these tech companies have, it will not be easy to achieve justice. The act, although worthy and necessary, is also more focused on protecting

---

* Lloyds Banking Group, "Two-Thirds of All Online Shopping Scams Now Start on Facebook and Instagram," May 30, 2023, https://www.lloydsbanking-group.com/media/press-releases/2023/lloyds-banking-group-2023/two-thirds-of-all-online-shopping-scams-now-start-on-facebook-and-instagram.html.

children than it is on protecting adults against fraud and is missing the victim reimbursement piece. There is still work to do.

Imagine the impact that could be made if these two powerful entities—banks and big tech—collaborated with each other. Currently, they hide behind data and privacy laws; these laws and regulations were not created to make it difficult to combat crime—they were created to protect the individual—and should not be used as an excuse to not share data. We know it's not as easy as we may make it sound; there are compliance laws and regulations these entities have to abide by. But what the UK's new legislation will hopefully lead to, with everyone sharing responsibility, is more collaboration. If issues arise that make it difficult to warn other entities of fraudulent accounts, they could put pressure on law enforcement or lawmakers to make necessary changes to laws or procedures.

Fraud needs to be addressed by a centralized organization, with the resources to take the crime head-on, in a holistic way. UK Finance, formed in 2017, serves as the umbrella organization and spokesperson for credit, banking, markets, and payment-related services in the UK. They can inform the banks from the top down. Currently, the United States does not have a similar entity that looks at the problem as a whole and implements procedures accordingly. This entity could require all banks to have a joint process for combating fraud; currently, each bank has its own set of processes, which may or may not involve contacting law enforcement.

With any other type of crime that we suspect or witness, it is understood that we have an obligation to call the police. Shouldn't we at least have a moral, if not legal, obligation to try to not let someone send money to a fraudster? It's like seeing someone getting beaten or abused and doing nothing about it. We need to look at fraud like we look at any other type of crime. And we need laws that hold the criminal and all major players accountable.

CHANGING BIG TECH

World Romance Scam Prevention Day was established on October 3, 2023. It's a day when social media platforms like to pretend they take precautions to protect their users. Tinder, for example, posted that they "care about your safety" and now have "ID verification check" to prevent users from being scammed. Their website states this "is an optional process that allows you to show that the photo on your ID, and at least one of your profile photos, looks like you." Did you catch that? At least one of your profile photos. What about the others? And what's the deal with making this "optional"? And besides, a user can use their real face to verify their account, then change all their photos to fake ones. The Tinder website admits that "this feature doesn't guarantee the validity of the ID or the safety of a particular user." It doesn't sound like they care too much about our safety, after all.

Still, at least some of the dating apps are trying to do something. The biggest player, Meta, hasn't done anything to stop the proliferation of fake profiles on its platforms. Search Facebook or Instagram for "Simon Leviev" and you'll find hundreds of fake profiles. People have created fake profiles of us, too. It is far too easy to claim you are someone you are not. Fake content has broader implications in society, too; it is heavily used, for example, during election periods to influence voters. There are even AI influencers now—virtual versions of social media influencers. These fake personas are appearing in ads, championing political candidates, and transforming the way content is created, consumed, and marketed; millions of followers are engaging with their content and purchasing the products they promote.

Big tech should protect us, but they're not. They were never there to protect us. They're not there to "connect us," either. We are just data for them; the more users these platforms have, the more money they make from ad revenue and selling our data to third parties. Plain and simple. The only way to make them care about user safety is to have the lack thereof financially impact them. If there are laws and fines for violations, they will pay attention. Without regulation, they have no incentive to do anything about criminals using their platforms, because they are making money off these criminals using their platforms.

Criminals are using AI and deepfakes—photos and videos of digitally altered faces or bodies or voices of a real person, or a fake person entirely—to better their schemes. As long as they have a sound bite of our real voice or a real video of us, they can re-create our voices and use it to call our mother, for example, and tell her we are in trouble and need money. With this technology, someone can hold a video call using a fake face and a fake voice. What kind of defense do we have against fraudsters with this type of technology available to them? How can we possibly know what is real or fake?

Software is being developed to detect deepfakes and AI-generated audio, but it is not yet widely used. Law enforcement isn't using it yet either. It's difficult to keep up with the speed of change, and the use of this technology no doubt comes at a cost. This is why awareness is so important; if someone gets scammed, it is not that they are naïve, it is that no one has informed them of just how much can be faked these days. We need to change how we view content online. It's sad to say, but we essentially need to assume that everything we see online is fake, until proven real.

One step we can take to protect ourselves is to conduct a *reverse image search* of profile photos or images used in posts to determine their original source—it may not match the source you have for the content. This will help you find manipulated versions or derivative works of an image. Tools to conduct such searches are continuously being developed and improved upon, so it's wise to do a search for the latest and best technology, but PimEyes is currently one that we recommend.

Of course, it costs money to implement safety and verification features. It's the biggest players, like Meta, that can afford to take that hit. LinkedIn has tried; they allow users to verify identity, workplace, and education institutions on their profiles, for free (some platforms charge for this feature). However, these strategies are not bulletproof, and there are tons of fake profiles on the professional platform, where people can claim they work at places they've never stepped a foot in. Most social media companies, however, simply say, "It's a complicated matter. We are working on it," and leave it at that. If Meta can create "smart glasses"—wearable computers, with augmented reality—it can certainly figure out how to verify people's identities.

If big tech isn't going to take this responsibility on themselves, we need laws that will force them to do so. It should be law, for example, that platforms can't allow users to misinform people with AI posts; any image or video or text that is created with AI should be clearly marked as such. Technology should—and could—exist that allows us to do an AI search to determine if a photo or video is fake; a program could be installed on our devices that automatically detects this for us and issues a warning. Why hasn't this been done already? We have fallen behind, but we can catch up.

CONVERSATION WITH A CYBERCRIME AND CRYPTO EXPERT: ERIN WEST

The increase in fraud is staggering, yet amid it all, there are people who are committed to making a difference. They're joining our fight, standing with us to bring justice and support to victims. Together, with these committed fraud fighters, we are finding hope and allies in places we may not have expected.

In 2022, Erin West, a deputy district attorney in Santa Clara County, California, founded Crypto Coalition," a network of two thousand members of active law enforcement from local, state, and federal levels and international partners who share cryptocurrency crime-fighting techniques. West first started Crypto Coalition to go after "pig butchering" crimes (a horrible name, we know). Like a pig being fattened before slaughter, pig butchering victims are manipulated into gradually investing more and more money into a fake investment scheme, usually through cryptocurrency. This is a clever crime, because financial investment is something the average person knows little about—especially when it comes to cryptocurrency. It is not uncommon to take the advice of a "financial advisor," or someone trusted to be in the know. Therefore, when a romance scammer is "dating" someone—often a targeted, successful woman with financial resources—who mentions they don't know much about investing, the fraudster knows they've found the perfect victim. Under the pretense of helping the victim make money for themself, it's easier to convince a victim to transfer money (to what turns out to be a fake account).

The group's focus has since expanded to include not just pig butchering but transnational organized crime, including sextortion and traditional romance scams. These kinds of crimes are so hard to prove, however. How do you prove intention? What if the victim's "boyfriend" was just a bad businessman? Because of the complexity of cryptocurrency and how fast it can change hands, law enforcement officials often brush such cases aside. In most cases, they have other crimes, "easier" crimes, they'd rather focus on. Which, in a lot of ways, is understandable. "Law enforcement is in a difficult place in the United States right now," West explained. "Police officers aren't well liked, and laws have changed that make it more difficult for them to do their jobs. Police departments are overburdened; they don't have time to take a burglary report or a stolen car report. If a victim can't tell an officer what happened to them in a couple of sentences and give the officer confidence that they'll be able to catch that person, then they're probably not interested in taking on the case."

West further explained, "Our society places value on arresting people who commit violent crimes, which we all recognize is important. Therefore, officers want to get on the homicide team or the gangs team, where they're out in the field looking for physical evidence. They don't typically come into the police force and say, 'I want to help victims of financial crimes,' which instead involves a lot of document review, compounded with the fact that it's a crime more often reported by women—a population that tends to be devalued.

Therefore, it's difficult to get this crime the attention and resources it deserves, despite the fact that investment and romance scams outnumber all other crimes combined."

Unfortunately, criminals benefit from jurisdictional barriers, lack of organization, and lack of ability to cross prosecute. "When you've been the victim of a crime, you have to get someone interested in investigating it and someone interested in prosecuting it," West said. If you get lucky and happen to get an officer interested in taking on your case, "not only do they have to prove something that is difficult to prove, but they have to prove it to twelve jurors who probably have some level of bias. It is a crime that not everyone is willing to accept as a crime."

What does all this mean? For one, victims have had to be their own advocates. They can ask for a financial crimes detective when they make a police report, but even that is unlikely to lead somewhere meaningful. "In my city of San Jose, with a population of nearly one million people, there is only one financial crimes detective," West admitted. "For victims, not only did something terrible happen to them, but then to expect them to be their own self-advocate in a law enforcement situation that doesn't want to help them . . . that's a lot to ask of a victim."

Which is why West started both Crypto Coalition and Operation Shamrock. Operation Shamrock, a collaborative initiative established by West in April 2023 to combat cyber-enabled crimes, brings in all the stakeholders, from law enforcement, banking, social media, telecommunications, diplomacy, victims' groups, and so on, and gets them talking to each other. "The best and brightest in this field have come together to volunteer their services to fight against this terrible crime that is wrecking people," said West. The organization also provides training. "We've had success in training law enforcement and banking representatives on how to talk to victims in a way that gets through to them. When they understand the psychological dynamic of what is happening to victims, they'll understand that saying 'you're being scammed' is not helpful; it will further isolate the victim and make them less willing to talk to them."

West explained some of the ways technology has fueled the growth of these crimes. Con artists used to have to mail letters to potential scam victims; with the advent of email, they could blast out hundreds, thousands, or even millions of messages at a time, dramatically increasing their response rate. Because of how fast communication is today, recipients take less time to consider whether they will click a link or respond to a message—a quick, impulsive decision might be all it takes to lose a vast amount of money. Now, with AI, a real person doesn't even need to send a message or carry on a conversation with a potential victim; bots can do this on their behalf. It only takes one human to monitor hundreds of bots, which exponentially increases the criminals' capability of accessing victims.

West emphasizes the international scope of these crimes. "It's predominantly been Chinese organized crime, but now we've got Korean organized crime and the Yakuza in Japan involved. Their tech is way ahead of us, and now we have physical evidence of what they're doing over there, with deepfakes and such. We used to be able to tell victims, if someone you've been communicating with won't give you a video call, you'll know they are fake. Well, now anyone can hold a video call and look and sound like a young, attractive Asian woman. That's scary and confusing for a vulnerable population, and even for the smartest among us."

AI can also be used to target individual victims. So much information about us is online; scammers can use technology to identify grandparents in a particular area with financial resources, for example, then use deepfake technology to call them and pretend to be their grandchild in an emergency situation. The possibilities are endless and ever-evolving.

"A lot of people want to brand AI as the worst thing that has ever happened, but it's only the worst thing that ever happened if only the bad guys are the ones using it," West said. "The U.S. Treasury Department is using AI to solve check fraud, which is fantastic."

West also believes that tech companies must be held accountable. Through Operation Shamrock, she and her colleagues are pressuring tech companies to take some responsibility. "It's taken a long time for me to just get them to listen. Now they're listening, but it's probably going to take an equal amount of time to get them to do anything. In the meantime, more and more victims are losing more and more money."

How do we further create change? West explained, "We've got to better educate and train law enforcement to understand that this is happening on a major scale and deserves additional resources to combat. We also have to change the attitude of society to destigmatize financial crimes and try to create a civilization that has empathy for people who have been stolen from in this way."

CHANGING THE LANGUAGE

One of the most important tasks before us is to change the language around fraud used in media and society, finance, and law enforcement. For media, it's important to be mindful of headlines, especially. We wouldn't say that someone "fell" for assault or burglary or anything else, so why do so many headlines say victims of fraud "fell" for a scam? By using the word *fall*, we are implying that the victim played an active role in the crime. We weren't "duped" or "tricked," either. We were targeted, then emotionally and financially abused by professional criminals, who are often part of highly creative, well-funded criminal networks. Our money was stolen, not given. We need to remove the stigma that victims are foolish or at fault and understand that this kind of crime can happen to anyone. Dr. Elisabeth Carter adds, "Public awareness campaigns need to harness strategies that would be acceptable for campaigns on domestic abuse and coercive control. They also need to use the words 'grooming' and 'abuse' and stop using words like 'scam' (use 'fraud') and 'fall for' (use 'become a victim of')."

In banking, industry fraud leader and practitioner Karen Boyer says, "Fraud is the new friction, and fraud prevention is the new customer service." When Cecilie was working as a UX designer, her job was to make everything easy ("frictionless") for the user—the fewer clicks, the better, in order to speed up how long it takes them to convert. Then she saw the implications of making transactions too easy, when she was able to take out several large, high-interest loans with very few clicks and very little friction. If financial institutions and platforms implement more healthy friction, they are taking care of us—their customer—instead of allowing us to lose money to fraud.

Banks need to ask their customers more questions when they see unusual spending patterns or a series of loan applications, and they need to do so with language that shows concern and care, versus accusations (for example, "We noticed unusual activity on your card. Is everything okay?" versus "We know you're not the one using your card.") The "5 Whys" method* could be used when speaking with fraud victims. By simply asking "Why?" about a suspected fraud victim's decision to make a transaction and repeating this question up to five times, it often reveals underlying motives or uncertainties. This approach helps uncover that the transaction may be influenced by fraud, as victims typically struggle to justify their actions under closer examination. Here's a sample script of what that conversation could look like:

> Bank Employee: Hi, [Customer's Name]—We've noticed some unusual activity on your account. Is everything okay?
>
> Fraud Victim: Oh, yes, everything is fine. I needed to send this money to a friend.
>
> Bank Employee: I understand. Can I ask why you needed to send such a large amount all at once?
>
> Fraud Victim: Well, they're in trouble and needed my help urgently.

---

* Interaction Design Foundation, "5 Whys," accessed February 20, 2025, https://www.interaction-design.org/literature/topics/5-whys.

Bank Employee: I see. Why do you think they asked you specifically for this help?

Fraud Victim: They trust me, and I'm the only one who can help them right now.

Bank Employee: That's thoughtful of you. Why do you think they couldn't ask anyone else or use another way to handle their situation?

Fraud Victim: They said their accounts are frozen, and they can't access their money at the moment.

Bank Employee: That's unusual. Why do you think their accounts would be frozen, and does this situation feel normal to you?

Fraud Victim: Well, they told me they're dealing with some legal issues, but now that I think about it, it does sound a bit odd.

Bank Employee: That's a good observation. Why do you think someone would ask you to send money instead of resolving these issues through their own bank or legal channels?

Fraud Victim: Hmm, I hadn't thought of that. Maybe it's worth checking with someone else about this situation before I send more money.

Law enforcement needs to treat victims with more understanding and compassion as well. When a victim has the courage to come forward and report the crime, it needs to be treated as a criminal case (a violation of a criminal law). So many relationship fraud cases, especially in-person ones, are brushed aside as civil (a dispute between private parties) instead. One victim we met said a prosecutor told her, "It's not fraud, because you knew the guy—he was your boyfriend." News flash: a person can be defrauded by someone they know! They're not all civil cases, some are criminal. It can be abuse.

When a case is looked upon with the proper language, it is taken more seriously by law enforcement and beyond.

Dr. Elisabeth Carter advocates for victims of fraud to be given an ABE (achieving best evidence) interview by law enforcement. "This is an interview where victims and witnesses of traumatic events, such as sexual assault or domestic abuse, are asked open-ended questions. Rather than asking, 'What did you do next?' which can revictimize someone and make them feel like they've done something wrong, they should be asked, 'Tell me about this whole situation' and 'How did you feel at that point?' This way, the interviewer can draw out feelings and link them to the harm done by the perpetrator, such as coercion tactics that the victim doesn't even know about." The benefits of this strategy are multifold. "It uncovers details essential for investigation and doesn't retraumatize victims; it shows victims that they are being listened to properly and that what they've been through is a serious crime."

A step in the right direction, she says, is that the City of London Police are all being trained as fraud officers. "Previously, that was a specialist role. Now they are all being trained to keep an eye out for interpersonal types of fraud." The UK could benefit, however, by changing the language around fraud detection campaigns. "The 'Stop! Think Fraud' campaign places the blame on the victim, rather than the criminal."

Furthermore, she says, "Support and aftercare needs to be more aligned with the established routes of aftercare for victims of other crimes involving grooming and abuse. All of these changes would make a huge difference in societal thoughts on fraud victims and perpetrators, and crucially would deliver support and aftercare that is much needed to fraud victims." When we view fraud victims as victims of emotional and financial abuse, government and society will also be more likely to offer them mental health services and support. Victims of relationship fraud need peer-to-peer support. Everyone we spoke to wants to connect with others who understand what they've been through and see that they're not alone. Victims become empowered when they come together. And of course, some victims need more than peer-to-peer support; being connected to a therapist who is trained in working with fraud victims can be critical to their recovery.

As a society, we're all part of this problem. No one should feel like fraud has nothing to do with them. It's in your backyard, it's in your room as you scroll online, it's everywhere. It's not something that you can escape. We all need to come together and do our part to help end the stigma and lower incidences of fraud. Just reading this book is helping! But don't keep this information to yourself; sit down with your grandparents or parents, children or neighbors, or friends who are online dating. Tell them what to look out for (a good place to start is the Resources section of this book). Knowledge is power.

If you've been a victim of fraud yourself, it's sad but true that you are the best person to see fraud in the future. Humans tend to learn best by doing. If you've worked for a global corporation, the IT department at your employer may have tested this theory out on you by sending fake phishing emails (if you click the link, you've failed the test). It's like touching a hot stovetop when we're little; we learn quickly never to do that again. Feeling something in our body (such as what it feels like to lose money) makes us more mindful in the future. We are also more likely to be informed, since we probably read up on the crime and experienced the systems in place (or not in place) to try to get our money back. It's our job, therefore, to share this awareness with others. To tell our stories.

Human stories help change the stigma of relationship fraud. *The Tinder Swindler* has been part of that change. It has given victims a voice. Our coming forward has made other victims less afraid to report the crime, to speak out about what has happened to them and to so many others. For those suffering in silence, seeing where we are today—that there is life after fraud—shows that victims can take back some control of the narrative. It starts by changing the language.

CHANGING OURSELVES

Cecilie

Once I went public with my story, I knew I had to do something more with the platform I was building. I wanted to be bigger than Cecilie Fjellhøy, fraud victim. If I created an organization, I would have a bigger voice and more credibility. At that point in time, it felt like no one was listening to me in my home country. I thought, if I could collaborate with others under the umbrella of an organization, what I had to say about relationship fraud might be taken more seriously.

That's when I met Anna Rowe, a victim of catfishing in the UK, who was already providing support and education for victims of emotional fraud through her organization, Catch the Catfish. We decided to join forces through our charity, LoveSaid. The organization is in the early stages of becoming a think tank for relationship fraud victims and a resource site and support system for victims who don't know where to go. We want to provide support for victims in the situation they're in and in the country they're in, since every country handles fraud differently.

Through the organization and through my own public speaking endeavors, I have been hired to give talks across Europe, the UK, and the United States, to audiences of all different types. The talk that made the biggest impact on me, where I most felt I had a voice, was with the UK police. To see police officers horrified when I talked about the treatment I received from law enforcement was so validating. I truly felt like they cared and would not handle things the same way with victims going forward.

Another significant talk Anna and I gave was for the UK Home Affairs Committee, under the House of Commons in the Parliament of the UK, that was conducting an inquiry into fraud. That felt like such a huge step, to talk about my experience as a victim in front of politicians who were going to create a report on the government's next steps in the fight against fraud. We served as experts, voices for other victims, for the government to understand the impact of fraud. Following our talk in Parliament, we even appeared on *This Morning*, a popular morning TV show in the UK. The UK has since come along much further than other countries, and to be able to be a part of that process is humbling and gratifying. We've also been on panels and given webinars for banks, including Lloyds Bank and NatWest in the UK.

While my work with LoveSaid is deeply fulfilling, my career as a public speaker has also taken on a life of its own. I've been invited to speak for a wide range of prestigious organizations, including the World Economic Forum, the London Stock Exchange, Gartner, and Mastercard. These talks cover topics such as relationship fraud, resilience, and overcoming adversity. Speaking to Mastercard, one of the credit card providers involved in my fraud case, was particularly powerful. They wanted to hear my story firsthand—not just as a statistic but as a human being impacted by fraud—to improve how they protect their customers. Their commitment to breaking the stigma and leading the discussion on fraud is inspiring.

At various other talks we give, people from Meta and other social media platforms are in the audience. I hope they're paying attention. We've had meetings with Tinder and Bumble, so their doors are open. Beyond all the education talks we've given to industry professionals, what really gets me excited is the peer-to-peer support we've been able to give, typically online. Fraud victims are the most qualified to support other fraud victims; we've been there, done that. We can heal together.

Take Pernilla and me, for example. Most friendships don't start the way ours did; we never would have met had we not been defrauded by the same man. Out of our trauma came a special bond that no one can break, because no one can take away what we went through together. Her voice was even louder than mine in the beginning, because I felt so broken when we first met. But Pernilla wouldn't let me give up. She was a strong, supportive presence in my life and a friend who truly understood what I'd been through, in a way no one else could, when I needed that the most. Finally, I had someone in this fight with me. Where we were then versus where we are now is miles away, and what we have been able to achieve would not have been possible if we hadn't been in this battle together. Having someone there to give each other energy when we're low has been so critical to pushing forward.

We have both become even stronger women as a result of what we experienced, but we still each have our moments. Our lives are so different now, with different challenges, but we can always count on each other to be there when needed. When I'm having trouble finding a flat to rent because of the bankruptcy on my file and bad credit, I can call her to scream and cry. When she's struggling with sick twins who won't fall asleep, she can call me to scream and cry. Life will always have difficulties to overcome, but we are proof that there is life after fraud. Maybe it's different than we had envisioned, but there is a life, and it can be a beautiful one.

At the time of this book's writing, I am thirty-seven years old and single. Some victims of relationship fraud say they will never date again, but that's not me. I'm too young to let one man destroy the rest of my romantic life. I just haven't found the right match yet. Sometimes people ask me, "When are you going to settle down?" The truth is, I don't know, and I don't care. I'm so happy with my life right now; I know I'm right where I'm supposed to be. Trauma teaches you to make the best of every situation.

Most importantly, I'm excited about the future. Working in the fraud industry now, I see a lot of good-hearted people across all sectors who want to do what's right and are coming up with solutions to difficult problems. Laws are changing, banking and law enforcement processes are changing, and technology is evolving to address this issue. The criminals haven't won. They got a head start, but we are catching up. Until then, we need awareness campaigns that make an impact. Storytelling is one of the best ways for a message to be heard, and more and more victims are finding the courage to come forward, partly because of the success of the documentaries we've been a part of.

Telling my story for *The Tinder Swindler* and for so many interviews afterward has not been easy; certain parts of my story still feel so vulnerable to tell. Sometimes I'm moved to tears, but to me, tears do not show weakness. To be able to go in front of cameras and bare your heart and soul is a sign of strength. It shows you are connected to your feelings and emotions, that you haven't dissociated from what happened to you. What is dangerous is if you don't feel anything anymore. As long as you're crying, you're still alive, still feeling, still healing. Still surviving.

Pernilla

After I was first defrauded, I was so angry with everyone—with Simon and his accomplices, the police, the banks, the media, and the public. I knew I was going to get run over by a bus when *VG* released that first piece, but I did it anyway; I saw the bigger purpose of going public—I wanted to make a statement that victims of relationship fraud haven't done anything wrong and shouldn't be ashamed. Still, I couldn't believe how mean people can be.

After some time, however, I realized I couldn't go around being angry my entire life, trying to be who I was before the fraud. I can never be that same person again. All I can control is what my life looks like now and going forward. The money I lost won't be returned to me from Simon or the banks, but it can be earned back in a different way. The emotional trauma I endured can make me a better, stronger person in the end—and already has. I can still fight against fraud and bring about positive change in society.

Technology is not just growing, it's exploding. What is happening with AI and deepfakes is scary and appalling. People are too money hungry; they invent technology without thinking about the repercussions of what they're putting out in the world. What do they think people are going to use voice-altering technology for? It's not morally right, and furthermore, it shouldn't be legal.

One of the ways I've channeled my efforts has been to collaborate with business partners to co-found IDfier, an app designed to address the complex identity verification challenges posed by emerging technologies such as AI and deepfakes. We created the app because we found it very hard to verify someone's true identity then peer to peer. While victims of relationship fraud are often blamed for not doing their due diligence, the reality is that accessible and reliable tools to verify online identities have been scarce.

IDfier is a proactive solution that helps prevent scams and fraud before they occur. It enables individuals and businesses to securely verify identities, mitigating risks associated with online interactions. The app utilizes features such as document capture, NFC (near field communication) reading for chip-enabled IDs, and facial recognition to confirm an individual's identity. There are so many situations when using this app makes sense: when starting to date someone, hiring a nanny, renting out a property, ordering items online through a secondhand market, or interacting with anyone online.

Before, I didn't really know what I wanted to do in life, workwise. I was jumping around between jobs I was good at but didn't love. But this, I love doing. I love creating change, making a positive impact in the world. I'm so proud of this company and the people I work with.

One of my dreams for the future is to open a rehabilitation center for victims of fraud, where they can gain access to lawyers and therapists who can help them rebuild their lives. It was so hard for me to find a lawyer in Sweden willing to take on my case, and equally hard to find a therapist who understood the crime that had happened to me. The first therapist I met with redirected me to a trauma center because they hadn't been trained in trauma-informed therapy. The trauma center therapist, however, said that what I'd been through wasn't traumatic enough to fall under their care. The third therapist I met with was more fascinated by my story than focused on treating me. I'm sure I could have found a good fit eventually, but it shouldn't have to be so hard. I'm blown away that, with fraud being one of the most common crimes in the world, government-founded mental health support for fraud victims doesn't seem to exist.

Making *The Tinder Swindler* ended up serving as therapy for me because, before shooting the interviews for the film, I was on the phone for hours and hours with Felicity and Bernadette, going through the details of my story. They helped me process what I'd been through, and for that I'm forever grateful. That was the beginning of my rehabilitation, along with all the love and support I received from some amazing reporters and viewers of the documentary who reached out to me. Despite some of the victim blaming we faced in the media, we received more love than hate. I know that all I did was try to help a friend. Is that so wrong? If I had had more knowledge on this subject, maybe I wouldn't have made the choices that I made, but none of what I did made me a bad person.

I lost a part of who I was and a lot of money, but I decided to let that go. The most valuable thing that we have as humans isn't money; it's our health and our time on Earth. If I let my criminal take even more of my time, I'd be letting him take my most valuable possession—and, in essence, continue defrauding me. I refuse to give him that power. Of course, I still have days where I can slip back into the past, but those moments are fewer and further between than ever before.

I get messages every week from victims (or near victims) of fraud, thanking me for putting my story out there. It either saved them from being defrauded or made them feel less alone. Just recently, I was at a restaurant when a woman came up to me and gave me a hug. "Who are you?" I asked.

"I'm so sorry," she said. "I just had to give you a hug, because you saved me. I was dating this guy, when my friend told me to watch your documentary. I watched it, and I realized the guy was grooming me to be defrauded. I later learned he had multiple victims. I don't know what would have happened to me had I not seen the documentary!" Those exchanges mean so much to me; they make all the effort and sacrifice worth it. If I can be the reason someone else doesn't get defrauded, or that they report the crime committed against them, then I'm happy. I dreamed of being Batman when I was a little girl; I wanted to fly around helping people. That dream has come true, just maybe not in the way I'd imagined!

I wish I hadn't been defrauded and wouldn't want anyone else to have to live through what I lived through, but in a way, I'm happy I did live through it. I'm not much of a believer, but I do believe that something bigger than me gave me this life experience. It changed my perspective on life; rather than get caught up in the emotions I felt in the beginning, such as "What have I done wrong in life to deserve this?" I now choose to view the experience as leading me to my purpose. My priorities are different now. I spent so much of my life taking care of others that I sometimes forgot to take care of myself. The Pernilla who said yes to everyone and everything no longer exists. Now I tend to my family and myself first, and whatever energy I have left goes toward my close friends and work that I am passionate about.

And that involves Cecilie, because none of this would have happened had we not been brought together, as one joint force, to try to make a difference in this world. I lost some "fake" friends when I got defrauded, but I found one true friend. I can't see my life now without her. You never know what's waiting on the other side of loss.

I'm not in a trauma anymore; I moved on. I have a beautiful family, and it's more important to me than ever to create a safer future for my children. I want to be a parent that they can look up to and be proud of. I have been a victim of fraud, but I don't want that to define me. I did a lot before the fraud happened, and I've done a lot afterward. I am a proud survivor.

CONCLUSION

We are all vulnerable to fraud; it's what makes us human. But as a society, we aren't good at placing blame where it rightfully belongs. This reframe desperately matters; if society isn't examining the right problems, it will continue to go after the wrong solutions, or none at all.

Confidence fraud, according to the FBI, happens to at least sixty-seven new victims every single day in the United States alone, with many more too embarrassed or ashamed to come forward. Even though confidence fraud and relationship scams are frequent, and even though some of Simon Leviev/Shimon Hayut's complex and manipulative tactics have been publicized, we still get questions regularly about how we let this happen. Yet no one seems to be asking how society has let him off the hook. (And not only that, it made him famous.) We're still in massive debt (Cecilie still has creditors after her for every last dollar), while Simon is partying in Israel, continuing to commit fraud.

Since day one of coming forward with our story, we've been asked all the wrong questions. Inherent in the inquiries posed by journalists, the public, internet trolls, and well-meaning friends are not only blatant misunderstandings about fraud but major biases toward women and fraud victims. Truly, it's shocking. Instead of questions like "Why didn't you catch him?" or "How could you let this happen?" people should be asking, "Why didn't the police do anything?" . . . and the financial institutions, the government, big tech, the media, and so on. All those institutions, at one point, knew of Simon's massive widespread fraud and failed to act. Instead, they pointed fingers at us and let it keep happening to more and more people. A lot of systems need to change in order to stop fraudsters from ruining more people's lives, which starts by asking the right questions.

There are countless victims out there who feel like they're alone in their nightmare. We know, because we still get messages from these women almost every day. The first thing we ask them is if they've reported the crime to the police, and in most cases, their answer is *no*. There's no one global number for how many victims are out there, but we'd bet that every single person reading this book knows someone who's been a victim of confidence fraud. Our hope is that this book will help get the right support in place for victims of fraud, an artistry as old as time, so that we can all be *Swindled Never After*.

At the time of writing, neither Simon, Avishay, Piotr, Joan, nor Claudia have been charged with defrauding us. The mother of Simon's daughter has denied any wrongdoing. Simon has been convicted in other fraud cases and currently faces ongoing legal proceedings for additional charges.

RESOURCES

The Samaritans provides confidential support for anyone in distress, struggling to cope, or feeling suicidal in the UK. (www.samaritans.org)

The 988 Suicide & Crisis Lifeline provides free and confidential emotional support to people in suicidal crisis or emotional distress twenty-four hours a day, seven days a week, across the United States and its territories. (www.988lifeline.org)

The AARP Fraud Watch Network's toll-free helpline (877-908-3360) has trained fraud specialists and volunteers who offer guidance you can trust, free of judgment.

The UK charity Victim Support provides victims of crime and traumatic incidents free support and guidance on what to do next. (www.victimsupport.org.uk; 08 08 16 89 111)

Cecilie Fjellhøy and Anna Rowe's organization, LoveSaid, offers advice and support for victims of emotional fraud. (www.lovesaid.org)

Anna Rowe's organization, Catch the Catfish, has a wealth of information for anyone experiencing fraud. (www.catchthecatfish.com)

Advocating Against Romance Scammers (AARS) was created to help bring awareness and convey how online romance scams have impacted the world today. (www.advocatingforu.com)
Do you suspect that someone you know is being defrauded?

Parents or friends who know their loved one is being defrauded reach out to us, asking for advice. They inquire desperately, "How do I make them see the reality of their situation?" Sadly, most people in these situations don't want to see the truth of what is happening to them. They want to so badly believe the lie, because it makes them happy—or at least did, in the beginning—and because if it is truly a lie, their life is probably ruined, and that is something they don't want to face. It's very hard to get through to them, even with proper evidence.

All we can tell you is to not confront your loved one in a judgmental or harsh way; you have to remain supportive and calm, even when your loved one gets defensive or verbally aggressive or attempts to shut you out completely. It can also help to have multiple people calmly speak to them, so they can't disregard what they are hearing as just one person's opinion. Provide them with facts and information, and let them know you'll be there if they need you.

Of course, every person and situation is different, so there's no one-size-fits-all solution. The people closest to the victim know what they need best.

ACKNOWLEDGMENTS

Cecilie Fjellhøy

What a journey! Words can't describe how it feels to finally sit with a copy of a book I believed in so much that giving up was never an option—a book from survivors of fraud to *everyone* out there, so that you all may better understand the seriousness and devastating effects of this crime. It was a tearful and difficult experience, re-living *again* the worst parts of my life, to get this story down on paper. But it's been so worth it.

I want to thank the incredible Rebecca Pillsbury, for being the amazing writer that you are. Taking this story and blending it with research has not been easy, but collaborating with you has been pure joy.

Thank you incredible Pernilla, for always being there for me and partnering with me on this amazing project.

A huge thank you to my wonderful co-founder of LoveSaid, Anna Rowe, for always leading the way and inspiring me to strive for more.

Thank you to my beautiful family—my mum, Toril, dad Ove, brother Martin, and sisters Julie and Hilde—who never made me feel ashamed and always made me feel they were proud of me. Thank you for listening to me when I've been at my lowest and when I've been at my best. You are my life.

To my amazing friends in Norway and around the world, thank you for filling my life with love, memories, and laughter. Your support has meant everything.

Pernilla Sjöholm

Writing this book has not been an easy journey. For me, it is a story I wish had never happened—one I sometimes try to forget. Confronting and sharing some of my life's biggest mistakes has been both emotionally difficult and challenging, but it is vital. It is crucial to break the silence and address victim shaming and blaming and to work towards a better future where we can understand and combat fraud more effectively. The process of bringing this book to life has been hard, but it has also been deeply meaningful.

To everyone who has ever offered a kind word or shared wisdom with me—I heard it all, and it meant more than you know. Your support and encouragement have shaped not only me but also this book. Every message and every word of kindness along the way gave me the strength to push forward, and for that, I am forever grateful.

To my children, Lia and Philip, you are my everything. Everything I do in life is for you—to create a better world, to make a difference, and to make you proud to call me your mother. This book is another step on that journey.

Thank you, Carl, for making me a mother and for standing by my side through the emotional process of bringing this book to life—your love and presence mean everything.

Thank you to my mother, Lena, and father, Per-Kåre, for always being there, for giving me strength when I needed it most, and for your unwavering support—especially in making this book possible. Thank you, from the bottom of my heart.

To my grandmother, Britt, and grandfather, Gert, for your endless love and guidance. You are the example I strive to live by.

Cecilie, my co-author, my friend—you have been my greatest support through everything. Writing this book together has been yet another chapter in our journey, and I couldn't have asked for a better partner.

Thank you to Rebecca Pillsbury, for helping shape our words and vision into something truly meaningful. Your dedication and talent brought this book to life in ways we couldn't have done alone.

ACKNOWLEDGMENTS

***

We would both like to thank Brandi, our book agent at UTA, for believing in this project, guiding us through the process, and helping turn it into reality. Thank you to the team at Podium for believing in this project and helping us get it out into the world.

Thank you to the incredible journalists in Norway, Erlend Ofte Arntsen, Natalie Remøe Hansen and Kristoffer Kumar, who were with us in the initial stages of creating the original *Tinderswindler* for the Norwegian newspaper, *VG*. Without your belief and understanding back in 2018, this book would never have seen the light of day.

Thank you to the incredible Felicity Morris and Bernadette Higgins, for creating the Netflix documentary and bringing the topic of romance fraud to the forefront.

A heartfelt thank you to our life rights agent at UTA, Addison Duffy, who recognized the potential of this story back in 2019, and to the incredible team at AGC Studios for being part of this journey.

A final heartfelt thank you to all the experts who contributed their knowledge and insights to this book—Daniel Simons, Christopher Chabris, Dr. Elisabeth Carter, Miguel Clarke, and Erin West. Your expertise has been invaluable in shaping its message and impact. Your voices are vital in the fight against fraud, and we are honored to have your contributions in these pages.

Cecilie Fjellhøy is an international keynote speaker on fraud, trust, and resilience. Originally from Norway, she brings lived experience and a master's degree in DXD (digital experience design) to her mission of building safer online spaces. As cofounder of LoveSaid, Fjellhøy supports victims of romance fraud and works to effect meaningful change. She advises organizations and businesses and consults on digital trust issues, driven by a commitment to systemic reform. Fjellhøy is currently based in London.

Pernilla Sjöholm is a Swedish entrepreneur, keynote speaker, and cofounder of the identity verification platform IDfier. After she was featured in Netflix's award-winning documentary *The Tinder Swindler*, she became a fierce advocate for raising awareness about fraud and empowering individuals to protect themselves in the digital world. Today, Sjöholm speaks on scams, digital safety, and women's empowerment, working to create lasting change and help others navigate a safer, more transparent world. She lives in Stockholm, Sweden.

Podium

DISCOVER MORE
STORIES UNBOUND

PodiumEntertainment.com

www.ingramcontent.com/pod-product-compliance
Ingram Content Group UK Ltd.
Pitfield, Milton Keynes, MK11 3LW, UK
UKHW042251110825
7345UKWH00003B/259